Business

Killers

Why Business Are Failing

Solomon Etchie Okpa

Business Killers:Why Business are Failing

Copyright © 2012 by Solomon Etchie Okpa

Unless otherwise indicated, all Scripture quotations are taken from the King James Authorized Version of the Holy Bible. All rights reserved.

Contents

Dedication

This book is dedicated to my late grandmother NENE, the three loves of my life – my mother, my wife, my daughter and to He, who owns me – **GOD.**

Introduction

My birth was recorded a few decades ago. But before my appearance on this earth I was in business, right inside my mother's womb. It all began with the formation of the foetus – that was my parents' business.

It was my parents' business to generate that foetus that became me. There, in my mother's womb, I commenced the first business, not without the aid of the organs that have been formed. Naturally, these organs were to extract fluids from the intake of my mother, mine was to naturally instigate them to carry out the task, until the time I was, by nature, due to appear physically. From thence I was introduced to the business world: a world where you must cry to be attended to; a world where you must labour to be fed; a world where you need not just yourself, but others too, to survive; a world where you cannot manufacture and produce all that you need to exist; a world where you must strive for honour and glory; a world where your choices are contended with by all. The list is endless – it is a business arena, with so much battle to fight; where no one comes out unscathed.

We were all introduced to this arena to contend for survival and existence. It is a scene where your survival depends on your versatility, a fast-paced world, where stagnancy is not tolerated, where there is no room for dormancy. You can decide to fail, or succeed. Your success or failure cannot deter others from succeeding.

Your emergence on the scene of life was with a task, and you alone must decide to carry out that task; whether for yourself, or others. This task must be done. It is the only one duty you have, and it is your BUSINESS. Your life on earth is a business; you were not just formed or created. You are not an afterthought, or a creature of chance. Your source is from somewhere. It was the business of someone – I mean your Creator, GOD. God is the first businessperson and He also, is the last Person that will remain in business. The details are in the first and last chapters of this book, respectively.

But what is Business? According to the Oxford English Dictionary: "Occupation, trade; task, duty; things that have to do with buying and selling, trade; commercial establishment."

The definition above is all-embracing; it cuts across any other definition that this term connotes, and runs through the gamut of personal skills to organization, operations and establishments. It further simplifies into retailing, zeroing in on activities like buying and selling – trade.

In summary, its composition is limitless as it has nothing to do with grade and hierarchy, but rather, it portrays business as an activity - an activity that is not limited, or restricted by any barrier.

Whether literate or illiterate, rich or poor, able or disabled, young or old, skilled or unskilled - business is an activity that all humans whether on earth or in the universe at large, embark on either for profit, or personal satisfaction, or for no reason.

BUSINESS IS AN ACT

This act creates the different class structures that exist on this earth. It is this act that differentiates the sexes –man or woman. It differentiates nations (industrialized societies, developing nations, underdeveloped nations). It also defines social status – rich, or poor, smart or, not-so-smart, skilled and unskilled: the list is endless.

True, as the above is, this act is unending, it is both spiritual and physical, and it has a divine origin. Divinity is governed by this act and parameters are in place to evaluate these acts. Life and existence is business, no marvel our existence terminates at death; this, by implication, means that business too, can die. Let's get this clear.

Life is equivalent to business; the measure of life is existence. Existence is evident by activities; on the other hand, whether it is done in harmony or disharmony, with, or without result in view, it must surely end in a particular way. This result is a function of how such activity is carried out. As long as there are activities with, or without an outcome, business is implied.

So if life equates to business that means all that affects life also affects business. This by implication means that if life ends at death so does business. Life can be taken (by death), business also can be killed, life improves so does business, and in fact the measure of life is the result of business.

This is a very serious issue, an equivalent that depicts the status of our existence. This implies that the level of our business defines the level of our life and vice versa. This also means that either of them controls the extent to which the other thrives. The success or failure of the other has a proportionate relationship. This means that your life which also is your attitude directs your business. This, in essence, means your attitude can either kill, or revive your business. In other words; your attitude could terminate your life. Take for example a man that is a drug addict, this attitude is a bad attitude and by implication, kills. Your attitude could be your killer, or your saviour. A poor attitude could give rise to a poor outcome, while a positive attitude would yield a positive result, just like the adage:

"YOU REAP WHAT SO EVER YOU SOW".

In the light of the above, this book focuses on things that are responsible for the death of business and things that could kill any business. The development will evolve from things that would kill a life, an evaluation that will be drawn from first principle, personal observation, experience and research.

You will be taken through series of issues that are killing your business; will kill your business or have killed some businesses. **One thing you would discover is that a thriving business now may actually be heading for the rocks, while the owner may not even know.**

You will also learn how to take the usual steps to preserve your life from harmful circumstances, that is, things that could kill you and how to apply these steps to protect and preserve your business.

One crucial lesson in this book is the equivalence of different levels of business; that is, the equation of small scale business to large scale business – growth and size are the difference – both could be killed by the same killers.

Just as we are surrounded by life-threatening situations, like volcanic eruptions, tsunamis, earthquakes, hails, floods, pollution and other natural disasters, so are our businesses.

While the book does not dwell on natural disaster, the focus is on things we can control; things that can kill businesses. These I call: **"Business killers."**

Business killers are all around us. In fact, one of such killers is always with us. This killer was with us when the first thought of starting a business came into our mind. It was this killer that at the instance of our resolve to do something, prompted us to start the business. Now you may begin to ponder why should this same instigator be the threat to the existence of our business? Who or what is this? The answer is in this book. The intent is to pave way for you to save either your thriving business, or dying business.

The assurance is that the book aims to prepare you for battle against these killers, so that your struggle will not be truncated and that your business life may not be destroyed. To aid this preservation battle, the book has been segmented into four parts. Part 1 focuses on the birth of a business; Part 2 focuses on the business assassins; Part 3 focuses on the actions of business killers, while Part 4 focuses on the last business.

You have just one thing to do now and that is, to discover why businesses are failing, so as to know how to preserve yours.

Please note that **my business** is to expose these killers to you, so that *you can protect and improve your business* – **this basically is your business.**

Solomon Etchie Okpa

Part 1: Birth of Business

Chapter one: The first business

We all know that space is needed to carry out any activity, and that all activities carried out equates one form of business, or another; some, without any definite result in view. Since we all need space to do business, and we are all in this universe, which happens to be the space. Whose responsibility was it then to create this space? Whose business was it to establish it? Surely, someone must have been responsible and that, by implication, was his business.

Though there are postulations that the whole universe just came from nowhere, and that all things began to evolve, until the more specialized organisms, like man evolved.

Logical as the above may seem, I am neither a follower nor a believer of that theory. My fault is that the order we see in the universe goes beyond natural control; there must be a force, and I mean, an orderly force somewhere controlling all activities in the universe.

The question is what is this force? The answer to this question will keep assailing man, as there have been different postulations, and theories by the scientists, philosophers, free thinkers and various religious groups on what this force stands for.

However, of all these theories and postulations, the most logical is the creation story as recorded in the Bible. The Bible is straightforward and specific on how the earth was formed. There was no vague description but specifically the Maker of the universe was introduced.

"IN THE BEGINNING GOD CREATED HEAVEN AND EARTH..." Genesis 1:1. This is the origin of the creationist postulation - God. To the creationist, the world, or the universe did not just emerge; it was the business of a supreme being, who thought out a programme and decided to execute it, which lead to the existence of man and his surroundings.

Recall, all activities equates business; this therefore implies that the first business ever embarked upon in the realm of human existence is the creation of the world.

The Beginning of the First Business
God started the first business. He did this in both a logical and a chronological order. We see divine intelligence in action, and we need to learn business logic from his action. Let's follow his order:

1) THE GREAT RESEARCH:

When you follow the process of creation, you would realize that God must have thought out the process before embarking on it. The reason, with all his power he did not create the world in one day. He must have done his homework, no wonder he knew where to start from - the creation of the heaven and earth.

The puzzle after this creation was that God knew and followed order, if not, why should a system be created from that which had no form and was void, with darkness "upon the face of the deep". We learn order from the process.

He was a researcher, so when confronted with this situation he moved around to conclude on the next step to take:

"And the spirit of God moved upon the face of the water…"
Genesis 1:2

With all the powers this great God possesses he still found time to investigate what he had created, he moved around to examine the specification before drifting to the next level to take the next action.

2) THE FIRST TIME AND ORDER:

God believes in process, he does not believe you should jump the gun. He works to create order out of a chaotic situation. As a researcher, when confronted with the situation he created, he drew up a programme.

We know God drew a programme from the logical way he followed through the process of creation. There was order. He knew what should come before the other. There was perfect order. No wonder, he did not create the organisms before creating water and light. With his research, he knew organisms would need both to survive. He knew the relevance of light and darkness in this creation process, so God said:

"Let there be light: and there was light..." Genesis 1:3.

He did not stop there, he knew the relevance of darkness, he knew what he had to create would need to sleep at some point in time, and that may not be very comfortable under light, so he created the first time:

> "And God divided the light from the darkness. And God called the light day, and the darkness he called Night. . ..." Genesis 1:4-5.

From the creation process, we know that God was working with a programme and he saw to the completion of each programme as documented in the latter part of verse 5:

"And the evening and the morning were the first day".

By these, the supreme intelligence knew what he wanted, he needed a means of measurement and eventually he created one - the first absolute time. This was because things must be measured.

3) CLARITY OF PURPOSE

We learn a very vital lesson from God's creation and that is clear; He knew what obscurity could cause but He needed to have a clear view of what He has programmed to create. He could have called for these things to appear in the dark and gloomy situation He was confronted with but His intelligence would not allow Him to do that, while His view in the dark cannot be separated from how He sees in light. For some reasons, He followed His divine order in that light. That is very important. To Him, there was no need for assumptions; He needed light for clarity on the process He had commenced, so he called for light – that means He called for clarity.

4) CLARITY REVEALS OBSCURITY

God truly is a Super-thinker, One that knows what He wants and how to go about it. The light, or clarity He created reveals obscurity, or things that naturally could have been hidden from Him. At dawn, He noticed what He wanted that hadn't been achieved.

The clarity he created, revealed an obstacle, His earth was waterlogged. "No way, this would not work" he must have thought. So he started the separation process, he divided the water into two, one to form heaven or the firmament and the other to remain on the earth. So he rested on that second day. Read Genesis1:6-8.

5) BUSINESS PURPOSE/SATISFACTION

God must have felt a great satisfaction for this business He had embarked upon. He must have looked at His program and realized that what He intended to create were not all aquatic – He was faced with this challenge on the third day. Quickly a decision was made.

"Let the heaven be gathered together into one place and let the dry land appear, and it was so." Genesis1:9.

God's business from inception had purpose and satisfaction in view. He was going somewhere, but the route to that satisfaction most be paved. If you follow the process of God's creation, His target was aimed at something, and that target was the focus of this business He started. It was the driving force.

6) BUSINESS SUSTAINABILITY

The business God has embarked upon was a business He desired to make a success of. The business must be sustained and that platform was well established.

The platform to sustain his business would need a solid ground to thrive, and to thrive on that surface, it must be sustained. So God's next focus was the sustainability of his business. He therefore divided the water from the land and eventually created the key source that would sustain his business – plants.

"And the earth brought forth grass, and herb yielding seed after his kind, and the tree yielding fruit, whose seed was in it, after his kind, and God saw it was good". Genesis 1:12.

After this, God moved to the next level. He knew one thing was for His business to be sustained, but the business viability and survival was paramount.

7) BUSINESS VIABILITY AND SURVIVAL

God in his infinite mind was after a thriving business which would be both viable and versatile. This business would need to work, and at same time rest and eventually would need a deeper rest – sleep, so he created the demarcation – day and night, with regulation. The moon and the sun were introduced. Alongside the aforementioned, living creatures were created – all aimed at the survival of his business. So the different organisms were created both in the seas and on ground.

8) GOD'S BUSINESS TARGET:

For five active days of creation, God's platform for His business was successful, but the target was yet to be achieved. It was the climax of his business – the reason he ensured all that would make this business successful were positioned. These include:

- ➤ Water
- ➤ Light and darkness
- ➤ Plants
- ➤ Aquatic life
- ➤ Aerial life
- ➤ Animals

So he summoned a board meeting. He was ready to make the final launch. Everything that needed to be done had been done; not only that – they were well done. They were all good, so a board meeting was summoned. And just as if to say: "Come let's launch our product" He called:

"Let us make man in our own image, after our likeness" Genesis 1:26.

This was God's greatest moment, the final product has been unveiled, and all that would sustain this product had been put in place. So the product was launched.

"So God created man in his own image, in the image of God created he him; male and female created he them" Genesis 1:27.

This was how God established his business. One should expect that after this God should rest. That was far from the truth.

Something must be done. True, a great business had been established. True, the target has been met, but something needed to be done. And so it was.

9) THE GREAT INVENTORY-:

From the chronology of God's creation, one would realize that after each process, God took time to assess His creation, and at each point he was satisfied. After all these, one would have expected God to immediately relax after attaining the main target of the business, but that was far from the truth. From the instant He created man, God took an inventory. He reassessed all aspects of his business. This is contained in Genesis 1:31:

"And God saw everything he had made and, behold, it was very good."

A great business indeed has been established by this Great mind; He had achieved perfection, in so far as the business he started could now run on its own, it was a finished job.

"Thus the heaven and the earth were finished and all the host of them" Genesis 2:1.

10) RETIREMENT- A MUST

With a great job done, the requirement is not just celebration; one needs rest; so was the first retirement introduced to this world:

"And on the seventh day God ended the work which he had made, and he rested on the seventh day from all his work which he had made." Genesis 2:2.

This marked the beginning of the first business, a great business indeed, one that was designed to succeed and thrive – a business that had all that was required to thrive and excel; a business automated with success; a flawless business made by none other than the almighty God Himself.

I wish at this juncture, to make it very clear that this business discussed was not the only business this great God embarked upon. Other businesses were concurrently running with this business – so there was some form of multi-streaming.

Chapter Two: The Death of the First Business

I wish to start this segment on a sad note, and also wish to use this as a note of warning, that: "IF A BUSINESS THAT WAS CREATED BY GOD COULD BE KILLED AND EVENTUALLY DIED – YOU NEED TO WATCH OUT: YOUR BUSINESS FACES FOES OF SIMILAR CAPACITY."

A onetime thriving business, good and loved by God, became a business He regretted setting up. It became a business that grieved His heart, why and how was this business killed and what led to the death of the business? Who was to blame and what was God's exit plan or escape plan? So many things were responsible for the death of the first business. Come on this journey with me, as we tackle these killers one at a time. However, we need to first fetch out some salient facts.

What killed the first business was created by the owner of the business. This is a sad truth, but His intention was not that this should strangle his business. For the success of this business, God took time to run the business and see to its accomplishment.

"And they heard the voice of the Lord God walking in the garden in the cool of the day." Genesis3:8.

That passage shows that God did not just sit in heaven to monitor his business, but he took time out to oversee how the business was running. There is a need to also note, at this juncture, that this business was established by God to meet his personal satisfaction. That was the essence of creating a dynamic being like Himself – different from the angels and other heavenly hosts previously created. He had created the angels as servants and remote beings – there was a great difference between Him and the celestial hosts dwelling with him in heaven. He needed more satisfaction from his ability, so he decided to recreate a type of Himself – a similitude; one that He could relate with on his own frequency; and a being that would be dynamic like him. The reason he created man with free-will unlike Angels; man was to be his very special product- He replicates a free moral being with the ability to make free choices. He wanted to see how He behaves and controls both his emotions and choices – so, for that very reason, he allowed what could kill this business to be part of the business – the intention however, was not to kill the business. Let's clarify that, and also see how this business was killed.

These killers could be divided into two, they are:

1. The Major killers
2. The Minor killers

The Major Killers

There are three killers involved in the killing of the first business in this group and as earlier stated, these killers were created by God, not that they should kill his business, for such powers were not given unto them, since he had earlier on empowered man thus:
"And God bless them (man and woman) and God said unto them, Be fruitful and multiply, and replenish the earth, AND SUBDUE IT: AND HAVE DOMINION over the fish of the sea, and over the fowls of the air, and every living thing that moved upon the earth.- Genesis 1:28.

So we see that God empowered man (his business) to stay alive, no matter how powerful the killers surrounding man were. The mandate was more powerful: SUBDUE AND DOMINATE. But alas, the business caved in to these killers:

(A) Free Will:

God in his supremacy has a characteristic that distinguished Him from the angels existing in His realm, and that major characteristic is the ability to decide freely on what to do – free will.

The angels of God lack this character. They are not free moral agents, and theirs was to render service to God and as earlier stated, they are remote beings. Man, on the other hand, was an embodiment of free will, unlike the angels, man was created with an evolving and dynamic ability that could not be predicted as God himself was.

As unique, divine and great that characteristic was, it played a vital role in the killing of the first business. This dynamism was a tool in man to decide and to make choices without necessarily taking orders from the Creator (God).

In fact it was how this ability will work that actually made God create man, and He was pleased to see man use it, which was evident in the apportioning of names to the different organisms created by God. He had left that decision to man - so man named all the creation and creatures of God.

God must have been very pleased by seeing the working of his well thought-out and well designed business. He could see himself in action – what joy he must have felt.

Let`s however tackle the other killers in this category before analyzing the roles each played in the killing of the first business.

(B) The Tree of Knowledge of Good and Evil:

The second killer in this category was the tree of knowledge of good and evil. This tree among others was strategically located in God's business; in fact, this tree was a key player to test the "free-will" ability in man. We know this because it was at the instant of introducing this tree to man, that God made man to realize that he had a CHOICE.

"And the LORD God commanded the man saying of every tree in the garden thou mayest eat. But of the tree of the knowledge of good and evil, thou shall not eat of it, for in the day that thou eatest thereof, thou shalt surely die" Genesis2:17.

As it were, man was introduced to a gun that was pointed at him. It was as if God was telling man that "this instrument pointed at you has the ability to kill you, but the power you have over it is that you are the only one that can press (push) the trigger for it to shoot." This decision by God was not strange to him, he already knew the ability he has placed in him (that is, man) so he was sure that man would not press the trigger. But alas the third killer surfaced.

(C) The Devil (Serpent):

One thing I cannot say here is whether God had warned man about the presence of a tempter (the Serpent) in the garden, though reference was not made to that in the Bible, but if one would consider the accuracy and details with which God embarked on this business, through to the creation of man, while having a successful business in view, it would be both wrong and unfair to think, or say that God did not keep man in the know that there was another killer in the person of Lucifer in the garden.

"Ye are of your father the DEVIL (Lucifer)...He was a MUDERER from the beginning..." (John 8:44)

To me, a thorough God must have briefed man on that evil presence; He must have also cautioned him not to listen to him, above all he must have also made it very clear to him that he (man) has control over him (the devil).

What a pity! Despite the security operatives and power this business was empowered with, it was killed by the combination of free-will, the tree of the knowledge of good and evil, and the Serpent. How? We shall soon find out.

The three of the aforementioned however did not kill the first business alone, so other killers aided this cruel act. This will take us to the minor killers.

Minor Killers

There are a lot of killers in this category, we shall analyze them one after the other, not necessarily in chronological order.

(A) Loneliness:

God had created Adam, and then added Eve as his helpmate; so they were, the first beings on earth – living happily together while God intermittently visited, to keep them company – they were his duplicate.

For some reasons, while Adam and Eve were enjoying themselves in the bliss of God, a fallen angel was somewhere scheming how to terminate this bliss. Only God knows how long he had been watching, not until the situation availed itself – loneliness. Adam had left Eve all alone, God also was yet to visit, so the woman was lonely and probably was in deep thought. She must have wondered how beautiful the Garden of Eden was. She must have also thought of the greatness of God and many other things which probably paved way for the next killer – Curiosity.

(B) Curiosity:

Curiosity played a major role in the death of the first business.

"What is so special about this tree that our creator has warned us to steer clear of?" Eve must have thought, so this curiosity led her closer to the tree of "knowledge of good and evil" – she peeped into what her eyes was supposed to be blind towards. This action brought into limelight the next killer – Attractiveness.

(C) Attractiveness:

Eve drew close to the forbidden tree and what did she see? Beauty! She was amazed how beautiful the tree was, the leaves must have been very different from the others, and the fruit it yielded were lovely. She was impressed and probably wondered why God would want them to steer clear of this element of adoration. While she pondered this over in her heart, the next killer set in - Doubt.

(D) Doubt:

The moment she started to entertain unusual questions in her mind about what God had said, this killer slipped into her. Now, she began to entertain doubt about the truth in what God had said about the tree. While she did that, the next killer quickly rushed into the closed door of her heart that has been opened – Rebelliousness.

(E) Rebelliousness:

Eve had gone close to a tree they had been warned to steer clear of, and as if that was not enough, she started fondling with the leaves and eventually she got hold of the fruit – "how lovely a fruit", she must have thought to herself. And while she thought upon the beauty of the fruit the next killer set – Disobedience.

(F) Disobedience:

Disobedience is an act of breaking stipulated rules and regulations - this was where Eve finally missed it. She took of the tree of the knowledge of good and evil and ate and when her husband (Adam) came, she gave him the fruit and he ate of it too – thus they were both disobedient.

Killing of the First Business

This section of this book is one of the difficult aspects in the cause of writing this book. As I write, my heart is heavy with sadness and my eyes are weak, as I consider the number of killers our forebears were confronted with in the Garden of Eden.

The truth is that with these killers surrounding our forebears, they (our forebears) had absolute power and control over them. It was quite unfortunate that they allowed their subordinates to subdue them. And sadly, these same issues have continued to subdue their offspring several generations after their death.

As their children, let's see how they were killed by the aforementioned killers. There is a lot to learn from that: there is always an enemy around us that is never happy with our progress!

Adam and Eve lately realized that a former being that enjoyed the very privilege they found themselves in was not happy with their joy. This kingpin knew that there was only one way to rob them of this joy; so, while Adam and his wife were enjoying, he was strategizing their downfall, and he summoned his army.

His first point of call was to use a very subtle beast, the serpent. Of course we all know the impact of subtlety. Let's analyze the characteristics of subtlety.

Characteristics of Subtlety
(1) Deceit

(2) Trickery

(3) Lies

(4) Hypocrisy

(5) Pretence

(6) Betrayal

(7) Fraud

The traits of subtlety are numerous and these were the traits the kingpin needed badly to carry out the very first murder. Read John 8:44 (…the devil …He was a murderer from the beginning).

If you consider the minor killers as highlighted you would find out that the first three minor killers were not of themselves evil, but they paved the way for the last three minor killers to set in, giving room to the impacts of the three major killers.

The ring leader of this team of killers – no one knows how long he has been waiting – but the moment he saw loneliness, curiosity and attractiveness take hold of the woman; he quickly possessed the subtle serpent to create doubt in the woman.

> "Now the serpent was more subtle than any beast of the field which the LORD God had made. And he said to the woman, YEAH HATH GOD SAID, YE SHALL NOT EAT OF EVERY TREE OF THE GARDEN? Genesis 3:1.

What a subtle way to capture a heart that was already curious; so the woman entertained this conversation and one thing led to the other. While the woman reiterated the commandment of God that the tree must be steered clear of, the serpent confirmed the commandment but this time with a twist.

"YE SHALL NOT SURELY DIE". Genesis 3:4.

The interpretation the woman sought-after, to confirm her fears was finally handed over to her, so she rebelled and consequently disobeyed God.

> "And when the woman saw that that the tree was good for food, and it was pleasant to the eyes, and a tree to be desired to make one wise, she took of the fruit thereof, and did eat and gave also her husband and he did eat." Genesis 3:6

Just like the tempter said, their eyes were opened, but this time they realized they had lost their eternal clothing of living endlessly. They had pressed the trigger God had commanded them not to press and the bullet had been released. It hit them so hard that their heart was filled, for the first time, with shame and fear. Of course if there is one platform death needs to thrive, it is the platform of fear. So death set in. The verdict was long and painful to the owner of the business, but it was a divine verdict that could not be altered – you can read through Genesis 3:8-19.The key verse there is 19.

"In the sweat of thy face shalt thou eat bread, till thou return unto the ground (die): for out of it was thou taken: for dust thou art, and unto dust shalt thou return."

What a terrible end to a business built by God, a viable business that became doomed to die. A business that was success-packed but faltered. A business that was to live forever, that was eventually killed:

"AND ALL THE DAYS THAT ADAM LIVED WERE NINE HUNDRED AND THIRTY YEARS: AND HE DIED." – Genesis 5:5.

What an intriguing story of how a thriving business was thwarted and eventually killed.

For now, I will take my rest from a further analysis of this story because my heart is bleeding. One thing I want you to note is that the core of this book is a product of this story. I know as human that you must be very sad at this point. So am I. The reason is not far-fetched — our sadness today is a product of the death of the first business.

Chapter Three: Starting a Business

The death of the first business ushered labour and work into this world. It triggered human activities today which equate business. From the analysis so far we know that everything we do is business – starting from our natural instinct of breathing, eating, walking, and whatsoever activity we carry out as humans. These are businesses, as long as that activity is aimed at a definite result.

Eating, for instance, sustains us as humans and preserves our body and our alertness. So we must eat to keep our body components active, vibrant and functional. So also is breathing. In fact death is a result of a terminated breathing, that is, the moment we stop breathing, we are dead. So the business in this regard is that we must keep breathing, to stay alive. The business of breathing is a general business that all humans are engaged in. If there is one business we guide jealously, it is the act of breathing, because breathing is synonymous with existence. It is important to note that as important as breathing is to our existence, it is sustained not just by the act, but by the intake of a substance – air. The mystery here is that with the numerous components of air – Nitrogen, carbon dioxide, etc, our survival solely depends on the intake of the oxygen component of air. If a wrong component is inhaled, death is imminent.

So the natural thing the body mechanism responsible for breathing does is to strive for oxygen, to keep us alive. But living itself goes beyond breathing, walking, eating and drinking. These activities are complemented by the concept we all know as work or labour.

Work and Labour

These two words are not strange to us. Right from our childhood, after having been weaned, we were introduced to this concept. It has made clear to us the significance of work. We saw our parents or guardians carry out activities from which they either generated money from or were paid for. We saw them wake up early, went out empty-handed and later returned back home with goods in their hands. We also heard them discuss payments and transactions that were targeted towards earning money. The realization all these created in us was that we must carry out certain activities to make money, so as to provide for our sustenance. This is the concept of work and labour.

Work and labour are synonymous. It is modernization that appears to have gradually substituted the word: "labour" with "work". And in recent times, labour seems to be derogatorily referred to as activities carried out by unskilled personnel or unskilled people. Whichever way we look at it, both are targeted at one end – sustainability.

Whether work or labour, the focus is the provision of income to sustain us; income to keep us going. So we work to stay alive. This is the primary concept and reason for participating in any activity that will sustain us as earlier mentioned.

Work/ Labour Vs Sustainability

To work or to be involved in any form of labour is seen as a means of sustainability. Some of us were told by our parents or guardians that we needed the aforementioned as a means of sustenance, so that synonym has been registered in our minds. That is, **WORK AND LABOUR EQUATE SUSTAINABILITY**

However true the above may be, it is not accurate. The reason is not far-fetched because over time the concept of sustainability has grown from merely been able to stay alive and cater for our families to staying alive, catering for our family with less stress or controlled stress with happiness.

SUSTAINABILITY IS LIVING AND CARING FOR OUR LIFE'S COMMITMENTS AND CHALLENGES IN LITTLE CONTROLLED WAYS, WITH NO STRESS AND AN ASSURANCE OF HAPPINESS.

In recent times work and labour have become intertwined, the object of which is to ensure sustainability, a merger that gave birth to the concept of employment. This concept has relegated work and labour to the background. The modern day trend of sustainability is now tied to the concept of employment. On a broader view, a merger creates a better interpretation – employment of labour to work and create a means of sustainability and livelihood.

Employment

Modernization revolves around the concept of employment as a major component of sustainability. This concept is gradually becoming a natural component of our human make-up. The concept of employment has grown to a height so much so that, it is almost more important than the survival of human race. So naturally, a lot of activities carried out by us are targeted at employment. We go to school, so that, we could be employed; we learn one skill or another, so that, we could be employed; we do a lot to make us qualified to be employed. Interestingly, most of us started out learning before we could notice the difference between our left hand and our right hand.

It is not strange that most of us now see employment as a means of sustainability. But it is strange to say that in most cases, employment has failed to fill the gap of sustainability. Having in mind the definition of sustainability in this concept, it is easy to see that a lot of people have been robbed of happiness by the very employment they laboured all their life to gain. So with man evolving, the search also continues and a new line of thought, though of the old path, is gradually been embraced and may one day completely dethrone employment from the enviable position it now occupies.

Own Business

The concept of employment is one concept that negates the original plan the owner of the business (that is, man) had. Man was originally created with freewill (ability to take decision on his own, without necessarily consulting others, or taking orders from them) while employment is the opposite of "freewill", which requires that you must act in a certain way, as stipulated by your employer. So to a large extent, your freewill is controlled by another.

This external control in most cases is very uncomfortable, considering the self-centered and selfish nature of man. Issues of abuse are rampant. Assault and undue confrontation are some of the major challenges faced by employees, and of course these breed dissatisfaction and unhappiness. So, the very employment that aims at sustaining us has robbed quite a lot of us of happiness, leaving behind sadness and sleeplessness. With these, a lot of people are now looking at the option of setting up their own business; with the thought and hope of gaining back their freewill and freedom – a trend that has become rampant. However a lot of reasons that transcend the recovering of one's freewill and freedom are responsible for this trend.

Reasons for Starting Own Business

To this point we have seen the role "freewill" and "freedom" play in this emerging system - own business. There are other reasons why people create their own businesses. You should, however note that these reasons are all focused on the three aforementioned factors –sustainability, freewill and freedom. Let's look at some others.

1) More Income

Today a lot of business owners or prospective business owners are driven by the desire to increase their income. Some have discovered that no matter the salary they earn, that overtime, their expenses exceed their income. So while some will retain their employment, they tend to set up private businesses, or practice alongside their regular job, so as to cater for the excess. In recent times, the concept of multiple streams of income has been taught as a means of sustainability – a concept that is widely accepted and even taught by some of the world's financial gurus.

So, with the quest to attain sustainability and meet with the demands exceeding their incomes from their regular jobs, a lot of people consider the establishment of their own businesses, as a means of curtailing the challenges and keeping afloat.

2) More Time:

I remembered when I resigned from my job to set up my private practice. Time and time again, I came in contact with lots of my colleagues who reminded me of the time I now have. Overtime, I realized that a lot of people set up their own business, not just for an increased income, but to have time to themselves.

This concept is a driving force, and if you ask some business owners today what they have gained by setting up their own businesses, a lot of them would attest to the fact that their greatest joy is that they now have full control of their time and are therefore, taking charge of their destinies. So we see a lot of people running away from the stranglehold of employment to set up their own businesses, in order to have full control of their time.

3)   Acquired Skills And Knowledge :

"Why work for another, to be paid when I can use my skill to make more money?" This is one thought that drives a lot of people into the setting up of their own business.

Overtime, the acquisition of skills and knowledge may lead one to the point where one feels that he could now run his own business. This drive may not be due to sustainability but a desire for personal freedom and the quest to make more money.

4)   To Be Rich Or Wealthy

A major driving force today in most people is the quest for riches and wealth. If you go through a lot of financial books today, the lessons are centered on formation of own business, or quitting your job if you must get rich.

This get-rich syndrome has taken hold of a lot of people (including this writer), and the realization is that ownership of business has been tied to wealth creation and riches. It is no marvel that in recent times, more and more people have bought the idea of creating own business for wealth and at all cost, wealth must be created and riches must be attained.

5)   Unemployment

"Why beg when I have my two hands and legs?" is a saying widely accepted worldwide due to the high level of unemployment in the world. So many owners or prospective owners of businesses today will tell you that their reason for setting up their businesses was as a result of the lack of employment. So why do I have to keep looking for a job, when I can create one for myself?

6)   Employers Of Labour

If you take inventory today or ask a lot of employees today if they like their job, a lot may give you an affirmative answer (which is half-truth), but deep within them, their desire is to start their own businesses.

So many people have vowed never to work for anyone because of the unpleasant experiences they were subjected to by overbearing employers. The simple argument is that: "If my joy is tied to this job, I'd rather be unemployed". But when their financial need is considered, rather than staying unemployed a lot of people start their own businesses. Take note at this point, that this attitude of employers is a major business killer – this we shall discuss later.

7) Greed And Covetousness

A lot of people set up their business out of greed or covetousness. Greed in the sense, that their drive is not only aimed at sustainability, but the thought of just making more and more money, which may not necessarily be, that they need the money, or lack it. They may have all the money they need to sustain them, but somehow, that urge to grab all makes the formation of own business the key to satisfying that urge.

Covetousness also plays a role in this regard in that some people go into own business because they see others do so, and may envy them, or covet their progress. So the thought is: "If I follow suit, I will make it like Mr. so and so". This urge pushes them to set up their own businesses. We shall discuss the impacts of this type of drive to business later.

Now You Are in It
Now you are in it, have your needs been met? Do you really feel the freedom you seek or the sustainability you desire – your main drive of setting up the business? I wish to let you know that most business owners today are far from achieving their dream of setting up their businesses because of neglect. You may begin to wonder how neglect hampers the progress of today's business. Read on.

The Neglect of Business Killers

A lot of us spend so much time thinking about how to set up own business, we spend so much time analyzing how the business will operate; we study all the books in business sustainability, we consult the financial professionals on how to run a successful business. We are even ready to spend all of our resources – financial and material resources, to set up our business only for the business, having been set up, we start struggling and even regret ever starting the business.

The reason for this is, because when starting the business a lot of us fail to make provisions for what I call business killers – a concept that has been neglected over the years. Your financial advisers will not tell you about these killers because they may not know about it, or they ignore it completely. Business consultants and other professional business advisers may do the same as well. The reason is not far-fetched, it is either they neglect it or a lot them do not even know about their existence.

Are you at the very point of starting a business, or have you already started the business? You need to know that the moment the first thought of starting a business came into your mind you unknowingly roused the sleeping evil known as *Business killers*. Just as you started the plan to set up a business, so do these killers plan to thwart your efforts; they spend much time planning the death of your business than you put into the planning and sustainability of the business. And just like was stated in the introduction to this book, the major killer was there when the thought of setting up a business was conceived.

So now that you are here, in your own business, you need to stop neglecting things targeted at killing your business. No matter the investment, or energy you put in at setting up your business, be informed that there are much investment and energy also in place, to aid these killers at truncating your efforts and subsequently, killing your business.

However, if you have already started a business, or you are considering setting up one, you need to pause at this juncture to consider these assassins. They are assassins because they are targeted, not only at killing your business, but you! And you'll recall how people have died naturally, or through suicide because of an ailing business.

Now let's consider these assassins, so you can foresee them, prepare for them and possibly avoid, disarm and kill them before they kill you and your business.

Part 2: Business Assassins

Chapter One: Assassin - "You"

One thing I want you to realize is that the very first killer of a business is the owner of the business. Now this may sound strange and I am quite sure nobody has told you this before, but now you are reading it – you carry an assassin within!

Well, before we delve deep into this, it is very important we know and understand the meaning of the word *assassin*. 'Assassin' is a word we rarely personalize because of its meaning – a killer. This is the simplest definition of an assassin. Now relate this to the issue at hand; you may recall that your first and very aim of setting up your business is to stay alive in a sustainable manner. True, but do you also know that by this very decision taken by you, as good as it is; you have also taken a decision to not only truncate it, but assassinate it? While you consciously plan and set up the business, alongside is your unconscious plan and strategy to kill the business. However, note that this unconscious plan in most cases may also be conscious, but you are the initiator of both plans to set up and kill your business.

A Call to Debate
You may need to answer these questions before proceeding

(1)   Why own a business?
(2)   What makes you feel you are ready for a business?
(3)   Are you physically, spiritually and emotionally ready to start a business?
(4)   Is starting an own–business the real solution you seek?
(5)   Have you all it takes to own a business?
(6)   Is your drive to own a business genuine or jejune?
(7)   What are the things prompting you to own a business?
(8)   Are you ready to own and run a business?
(9)   Do you really believe in the business?

(10)   The tools, the personnel and gadgets around you; are they the right accessories for the business?

(11)   Will what you consider to be strength, backers and support, remain with you in and out of season?

(12)   Why this business?

Your answers to these questions will reveal the killer in you. You may not know that there is a killer in you; the truth is that any action embarked upon is, in most cases, your creation, and if the result of such action is fatal, then you have killed yourself. It's just like intentionally drinking poison or taking one's life. You are responsible for the death of "You". In essence, you have committed suicide. You are your own killer.

Where are we going? You may ponder. The truth is that it is not only when we take, or make negative decisions that are fatal that we threaten our lives; some decisions we take, like setting up own business – though positive – could also have a fatal impact on our lives. If not, why should a thriving CEO commit suicide because of his ailing business? Does that mean that the business he started was bad? The truth here is that such action must have resulted from the motive of setting up that business. So what are your answers to the twelve questions asked? Let's get the killer – 'you' from those questions and their possible answers.

1.   Why Own A Business?
What are your answers to the following questions?

(a) I want more money.
(b) There is no job.
(c) I believe I would be made rich from own-business.
(d) My job is no longer favourable.
(e) My employer is unbearable.

These are probably answers you may have given to that query – as genuine as those answers may seem; in them exist what I term: "assassins".

Let's consider the first answer to buttress. Fine it's great to enter a business with the thought of making money – it is a great idea – but one thing that desire fails to make provision for, is time and we all know that regardless of our mastery of time, we do not have absolute control over it.

So when you enter a business with the sole aim of making money, imagine if within the very first second up to the tenth year all you are doing is investing (spending) money in your business without any returns (profit), what do you think will happen to that business? A lot of people will abandon such business and may not wait for as long as ten years. Now, what do you think they have done to that business? Of course they have killed it.

Here is a puzzle: Do you know that some of the thriving businesses today were one time or the other started by someone and later on abandoned but yet that same business that died in the hands of one individual is thriving in the hands of another individual? So, when you start a business with money in view, without time in focus, you have not just started a business, but you have just killed one.

Again when you start a business out of frustration, because there is no job, what happens the moment you start your own business and you are confronted with that very job that had eluded you to the point of setting up a business? Confusion sets in. So while running your business and the thought, that you could be working for someone who would be obliged to pay you at the end of the month, no sooner then you start such business, you start looking for job unconsciously – this misdirected focus, has killed a lot of businesses and it will kill your business if you let it. In other words, you are responsible for that action.

In my years of employment, I came across a lot of people that quitted their job to run their own businesses, no sooner had they done so and we thought they had left for good than they re-surfaced, pleading for the very job they left. The reason for this is not far-fetched. The moment their expectations for starting their own businesses is not met, they remember their former place of work and the fear of failure lures them back to the same job they had abandoned. Countless number of people fall into this category, meaning that countless number of businesses have been killed in this way.

You need to analyze your reason(s) for opting for your own-business. You need to be very sure of the reason for your action, because one sure reason why your business will die is running a business with confusion, lack of focus, impatience and having time in-view.

One thing I want to assure you is that, if you focus on the reason for starting a business, without necessarily binding it to timelines, you will not fail. You must be ready to go the extra mile. You must be ready to reach the point where you have done all – assuming your business is not yielding expected results. But do you know that it is at that point that the seed (business idea) earlier sown dies, to pave way for its germination? Unfortunately, at this point a lot of people quit the pursuit of their businesses. No marvel then, years later, someone, somewhere, picks up such challenge and thrives with it.

2. What Makes you Feel you are Ready for Business?
What are your answers to this query? That same thought that prompted you to start a business in the first place might be the same that weakens you to pursue the business to a logical

conclusion. At one time, you felt you were ready, and yet, at another time, you felt you were not.

A lot of people, after due consideration of their knowledge, skills and finance, feel that they are ready for a business, but soon after they had begun, they then discovered their lack of preparedness. The truth is that, their readiness was not thoroughly examined before they embarked on the business in the first place. They started the business only to realize that they couldn't convert their knowledge, skills and finance into the very gains they foresaw.

It may not be that they were wrong in starting the business, but they may have failed in the perseverance test. The advice therefore, is that before delving into business because of your resources, take into consideration, perseverance, which is a function of time – you must be able to evaluate yourself in terms of patience to ascertain your readiness. This goes beyond the availability of the resources you possess. Your readiness is a measure of your perseverance and patience.

The lack of these two traits has killed a lot of businesses that naturally should thrive, and they emanate from us.

3. Are You Physically, Spiritually and Emotionally Ready to Start A Business

Starting a business, is not a thing you should toy with, you just must be ready before you delve into it, because the challenges of own business are enormous.

You have seen that your feelings are not sufficient enough for you to embark on a business, your readiness is paramount or else you will kill your business.

You kill a business when your entrance into the business is not physically, spiritually and emotionally guaranteed. Let's consider these three tools.

(A) Physical Readiness:

The success of a business is a product of the foundation. In this instance, the foundation of every business is the business owner, which you are. Your totality determines the survival of your business. Your personality is a reflection of your business.

So you may be wondering on the role your physical readiness plays on your business. Then, consider this example: Assuming you run a small restaurant, and as a person, you are unassuming, moody, sluggish and sleepy; imagine how that restaurant will look like. The obvious fact is that such a restaurant will reflect the outlook of the owner. The truth is that such an outlook does not portray the restaurant in good light. The cumulative effect is that, it cannot attract customers. You know as much as I do, that a business that lacks customers will one day die.

The inference here is that, if physically, your attributes are poor; your business output will be poor. This is a rule. So, starting a business with a poor outlook, will not only truncate the business, but you have, with your hands, set up a system that will eventually kill the business.

(B)Spiritual and Emotional Readiness:

This refers to your inner make up – things not seen. These include your beliefs, thoughts, desires, likes and dislikes. When these are not considered before embarking on a business, that business is bound to fail. Take for example, a man that does not believe in the intake of alcohol and cigarettes, and while his faith would not permit him on these; such person goes into a business that involves the taking of alcohol and smoking of cigarettes, you can imagine how such a business would end up.

What is suggested here is that, your spiritual and emotional well-being are *keys* in the setting up of your business. Be sure, before embarking on a business, that the business does not conflict with your belief, or emotion. A lot of businesses have suffered setback, because mid-way into the business, the contradiction surfaces – things the business owners dislike, are now part of the business. So, with their hands, they limit, and at the same time kill their businesses - a lot of people, quit at this point and as such, the business dies.

At this instance, you need to be very sure of your physical, spiritual and emotional state before embarking on your own business, lest you kill your business with your hands.

4. You Starting Your Own Business, is it the Real Solution you Seek?

In the part of the world where I come from, children are used to rate a marriage; so a marriage blessed with a child (or children) is adjudge to be a successful marriage, while the contrary is the case for the one that lacks the fruit of the womb.

Let's bring this to your business. Could it be that the solution you seek drove you to set up your own business? The truth is that most businesses are set up with a result in mind. So, you started your business from the onset with a particular result in mind. I wish to inform you that as good as setting up a business, with a particular result in mind may be, you need be warned, that your entrance into a business with this mindset could also be your undoing.

The question therefore, is: Have you taken time to examine all the options, to be way sure that your targeted outcome would result from the business you have chosen? The reason is because you can only take a horse to the river, but cannot force it to drink water. That lends credence to the fact, that certain result cannot be forced out of certain actions.

If you seek joy as a result of engaging in business, be sure, you are into what you can naturally do for free. If you seek multiple streams of income, be sure of the business you embrace. If you do not like crowd be sure not to embark on a business that involves your interaction with many people because while others would rate your success on a positive side you may not be fulfilled no matter the number of awards of excellence you are given.

The advice is that, you only know what you seek from a business. Do not start a business that will not meet that need, lest you will run a business that will suddenly come to an end.

YOU MAY BE GIVEN AN AWARD FOR RUNNING A SUCCESSFUL BUSINESS AND YET NOT BE FULFILLED.

5.   Have you all it Takes to Run a Business?
The greatest Man of all times in one of His teachings cried:

"For which of you intending to build a tower, sitteth not down first, and counteth the cost, whether he have sufficient to finish it lest hardly, after he hath laid the foundation and is not able to finish it, all that behold it begin to mock him, saying, this man began to build, and was not able to finish". (Luke 14:28-30).

Jesus knew the value of evaluation before embarking on a mission. You must be quite sure of the requirements of a business before embarking on it. Most of the businesses that have failed are businesses started without thorough evaluation and costing. You must, at the first instance, sit down and count the cost, if you don't want to quit mid-way into the business.

When you start, or enter a business without taking into consideration cost and proper evaluation, what you have done is to create a business that will die, and you are responsible for that.

Your skill, finance, knowledge and resources may not be sufficient for you to embark on a business. In as much as you don't need so much to start a business, you must be sure you have enough, to own a business if you don't want to end up a laughing stock.

6. Is Your Drive to Own a Business Genuine or Jejune

What is it that has driven you to own a business? What is that drive? You must thoroughly examine that drive, to ascertain its genuineness or jejuneness. Is the drive real, genuine, fake or jejune? What is that quest in you? The truth is that you need to be very sure of your drive so that it does not take you unawares. Are you profit-driven? So what happens, when the first few months you start the business profit is not coming in? What happens to your business? A lot of businesses have folded up because the drive that was profit-oriented was not immediately satisfied and as such, exiting the business was the next thing – they quit. The question is, why quit a business because the profit you anticipate isn`t coming? It could be that what ought to have been done to create such inflow of profits have not been done. Alas, you kill your business because of that unsatisfied drive.

Are you fame-driven? So, your music, or book has failed to bring you the fame you desire, as such, you quit and kill your business? You need to be sure of your drive, and be sure, that drive would be satisfied by the type of business you have chosen, or else, you would start up a business that would not last. So, whatever the drive may be, you need adequate inventory, and research to ascertain what can gratify that drive, so that you don't embark on an endless and frustrated journey – which has killed a lot of businesses.

7. What are the Things Prompting You to Own A Business

This is quite different from drive, or urge. These things may be words spoken by a relation, friends, associates, or acquaintance. These things may have entered you from external sources, or may just be part of your make-up. You need to be sure of your promptings, because one sure thing that kills business is that initial excitement to start a business without proper analysis. The truth is that, one could be talked into business. This may work, but the snag is that, when such fails, you tend to blame the source of the decision.

So before embarking on a business, you must be sure the decision is not only sourced out of promptings, but that they are solely yours. The reason for this is that, when the challenging and austere situations surface, you will be more likely to stand and face the challenges, knowing full well, that the choice to engage in business was made solely by you and not because you were cajoled into it.

The advice therefore is that you may be prompted to embark on a business, but be very sure the decision to embark on it is yours. The reason for this is that there is power when a decision to embark on a certain thing comes from within. These control your zeal and one sure secret of a successful business is your zeal. Your decision controls your zeal, whereas promptings motivates you but may not necessarily control your zeal. So check your business. The failure might just be due to lack of zeal.

WHEN YOU ENTER INTO A BUSINESS WITHOUT ZEAL THE BUSINESS IS BOUND TO FAIL AND DIE.

8. Are You Ready to Own and Run a Business

You may already be in a business or you may be considering setting up one. The question therefore is: are you ready to own and run that business? One thing you must note at this point is that to set up a business is one thing, owning and running that business is another. You may have the resources to set up a business but you may not have the ability to own or run that business.

The reason why a lot of businesses die today is because such businesses are run and owned by the wrong hands. What you need to understand here is that you may have the fund to start a business, but you may not necessarily be a good entrepreneur. So check yourself, check your business, you may need to free yourself from owning and running the business or else both the business and the resources you have invested into it will go to waste. You may need to delegate or relinquish control over the business.

When you are asked to relinquish control over the business, that does not mean you should give out your business, but rather hand over your authority to a competent hand to run the business, you would be surprised to see the revival of your ailing business.

The advice therefore is that you need to check the state of your mind to ascertain if you are ready to own and run a business, because you may not be so talented. One thing you need to consider at this junction is that you may have the ability to own a business but lack the ability to run that business. So what you need to do is to get a competent hand to do that for you, lest you kill your business with your hands.

9. Do You Really Believe in the Business?

Due to situation of things surrounding us, a lot of us have entered into one form of business or another; a credit to the situations surrounding us.

So, what we see around us are people involved in one form of business, or another – not out of interest but for the quest to survive. The implication is that, we are surrounded by people running one form of business, or another without actually believing in it.

You may need to examine yourself at this stage to ascertain your true state regarding your business. The big question that you must answer often is: DO YOU BELIEVE IN YOUR BUSINESS? It is certain that if you embark on a business you do not believe in, that business will naturally and automatically fail. The reason for this is that your belief controls your drive and your drive, as earlier stated, is a key to a successful business.

You may need to examine your belief in your business – the advice is that you quit that business you do not believe in, because a lot of the failed businesses in the world were run by men and women who do not believe in them. Your ailing business may just be a function of your ailing belief in the business. Quit, or start believing in it.

10. The Tools, the Personnel and Gadgets Around You; are they the Right Tools for the Business?

Is your business ailing and you have tried all you know to revive it, but the road seems blurred? Have you examined the tools you have chosen to use?

One thing I want you to realize at this juncture is that if the tools you have chosen are not the right tools, they could be classified as your business killers. So, if the tools you chose for your business is now the reason for the gradual death of the business, no one, but you is to blame. This is because you made the choice (of the tools) and as such you are responsible for the problem threatening to truncate the survival of the business.

You may need to examine the personnel and gadgets you have chosen for your business (we shall discuss these in subsequent chapters). This is because you could have chosen a hater of that business as a staff, and when personality that hates a certain business is projected as the business promoter, that business will not only fail, but will die.

11. How Committed are Your Strength, Backers and Supports?

Your strength may be your desire, your backers may be your resources, and your support may be your will. How strong are these to aid your business? A loose will could render your business directionless; laxity or delay will kill your business. So you need to re-examine your stance on your business. Your strength, backers and support are you and your mindset. You need to continually ascertain their status; else, your business would be drained of life.

12. Why this Business?

If you have read this book to this point, you might be wondering whether to stop, change, or strengthen your business. The last question is very pertinent to you, as a business owner. This is because the answer to this question is a core determinant of whether you are ready to enter into a particular business, or you are ready to improve your business. So answer this question honestly. You need to know that, should you not be able to proffer an answer to this question; no matter the business you are in, or what you intend to enter into (apart from the fact that you are not ready for that business), it will fail because you will kill it by yourself .

I do not have the answer as to why you want to start that very business, or why you are in that very business, because my business at this point in time is to introduce you to what I call "business killers". You need to know the reason for the choice of your business.

YOU NEED TO KNOW THE REASON FOR THE CHOICE OF YOUR BUSINESS

The aid I can give at this juncture is that you list out all the reason that makes you think you own a business or you need to own a business. After having done that, align it with the twelve ways highlighted through which you can kill your business, then proceed to the **subsequent chapter to examine external factors tagged as "BUSINESS KILLERS".**

Why this business? With the exercise on this completed, you need to forge ahead to identify other killers, so as to save your business, ailing business, or yet-to-be- established business.

Chapter Two: Faulty Business Foundations

So, you think you can appease God with your tithes and offerings after stealing, or robbing someone, or looting public funds? You lie. On this note, let's delve deep into the issue at hand as we tackle this business killer: "faulty Business Foundation".

Your business will die if the foundation on which it is built is faulty. Let's analyze some of these faulty business foundations, their sources, consequences and remedies.

1. Stolen Funds

As a young man, I have taken much of my time to study the world's billionaires, and in all these studies I am yet to come across a billionaire, whose business empire was created through stolen funds.

So the question is: Where are the looters, thieves and con men? How come is it that with all the money they stole, they are yet to be classified among the world's richest men? What do they do with the stolen funds? Guess what I discovered? These people also set up one form of business, or the other, but because the resources (money) with which they set up such businesses were stolen, their business can only thrive on stealing. So, the only way they can sustain such business, is by continual stealing. Their dealings are never transparent; their cohorts are men and women of like minds. One thing you need to know and note is that when we talk of business, we are talking of a system that has addition, subtraction, multiplication and diminishing effect; all these parameters can be measured. If so, how do you measure a business founded on money that cannot be traced to a definite source, or accounted for?

This kind of business does not have a route. Their sources are usually the owners and when you probe further into their source of wealth, you find that the monies were stolen. Please, follow through with your intellect:

How do you expect a man that stole to improve his business? The answer is simple: steal again.

So, a business founded on stolen funds sustains itself through stealing and continual stealing. Such a business cannot stand the test of time because its customers are either helpless or taken unawares. Again, if you had con someone into giving you his money, tell me how the business you set up with that money can thrive?

Let's consider our definition of the essence of business in retrospect – sustainability with happiness. You may wish to know that a man that is restless cannot be happy and if all you do to sustain yourself is to forcibly collect from another – you cannot be happy. The inference therefore, is that businesses that are founded on stolen funds cannot meet with the definition of sustainability and happiness.

Take note at this point that when your business is founded on stolen funds, business killers are endless.

(a) **God:** The creator of heaven and earth would be your very present enemy to trouble and frustrate you. God has access to our minds and He knows that the only way a man could be happy is via peace of mind. So He starts the battle within you. That's the reason such people go into drugs. The only way a restless mind can sleep is to either appease God, or go into drugs. For a thief, the latter is what he resorts to always. You know what? Problem is not what physically troubles us. The worst is restlessness of our hearts and minds. No matter your attainment in life, once you have no rest in your mind, peace will continually elude you.

(b) Invaders:

A business that is founded on stolen funds would continually be bedeviled by invaders. These invaders are like flies that are attracted to filth. These invaders are like rodents – uninvited guest to the house. Theirs is to steal and cart away resources they are not entitled to. The reason for this is that, the owner of such business may not have the eyes to detect fraudsters and may involve them in his business. Because of his ways, such are the stuff, his business would naturally attract.

What you need to realize at this juncture is that the reason why such business cannot stand the test of time is because its sustenance is dependent on continual and perpetual stealing. You may begin to wonder how. The reasons are numerous. Such businesses are projected in such austere condition that even workers are not well paid and if they are paid, the owners of such businesses create rules and regulations that may rub staff of part of their money (salary). That is not all; conditions of service in such organizations are stringent and inhuman.

2. Deceit

Is your business founded on deceit? No marvel it is not progressing? Deceit refers generally to falsehood, anything at variance with the truth. Simply put – telling lies. What would you say your business is rested on? Could it be that you have lied and deceived yourself and others? One thing to note is that a business founded on deceit would eventually crash.

Here is how it works: You have decided on a particular type of business, discarding every parameter that points to failure, should that business be embarked upon. Trends are drifting from that direction; the news about such business is self-evident and repulses one from its realm. Truth is: you don't need to go with the crowd; safety advices that you study the situation to fully understand the mood of the crowd and trends.

How about your perception, research and investigation on that line of business that discourages you from embarking on the business? So if you choose to discard the findings of others, what about your own findings. Alas! If you are hell-bent on venturing into such business, failure is imminent and the business would suddenly die because you have failed to listen to the voice of reason and have chosen to deceive yourself.

On the other hand, you may have cajoled someone to ply that route with you, knowing full well that the business will fail, but your plans are already laid out – you intent are to eventually take over the business. This is deceit. Ownership of a business by falsehood will not only lead to failure; the business will one day come to a sudden end.

You may begin to wonder why businesses founded on deceit will suddenly come to an end, the reason is because the foundation of that business is deceit and the thought of that alone would affect your mindset about the business. One thing you would realize is that, your thought would always point to the fact that the status of your business is not credible and so, no matter the transactions and the deals. The thought that you are where you are, is a product of deceit will not give you the required satisfaction. This may push you to be very inhuman in your dealings with your clients and your staff.

You know as much that, unhappy clients and staff kill a business quicker than bankruptcy - the reason being that, the route to bankruptcy is paved with dissatisfied clients and staff. By inadvertence, you may end up putting your partners and yourself in a racket.

3. Faulty Business Models (Preparations)

A business model is a flow chart that trails the path of a business through basic requirements, structure, distribution, marketing and profit. It is a type of preparation on how the business will work. A good business model is that which must be realistic, your zeal and vision of your business must not override your business model. You must be able to key honestly into your business model.

It is good to have profit in view, when starting a business. But the truth is that a lot of businesses ailing today were those founded purely on profit without taken cognizance the workability of the business. What you would realize here, is that in a good business model, revenue and profit comes last in the design. But what happens when you start your business with profit and revenue. The tendency, when doing this, is that, you tend to overlook some key points and strategies. So, you naturally plunge into the business for gains.

The aforementioned analysis explains the reason why a lot of people commit one crime, or another. They allow the gains, the pleasure or grandeur of such act to override their sense of reasoning and honour, while disregarding the consequences that may follow if they are apprehended. What such people have simply done is to start their business model with profit, discarding other working parameters. Is your business ailing? You may need to revisit your business model. In some cases, it may be your preparations and analysis that are faulty. Is the profit you sought for before entering the business elusive? You may need to overhaul your business strategy.

Just like a criminal whose life would be brought to an abrupt end when caught, so a lot of businesses have been brought to an abrupt end because of a faulty business preparation or model. You may need to rewrite your business plan if it must be rescued from the threat bedeviling it or from the hand of this killer. The right thing to do is to write a long list having profit at the end of that list. This action is very tedious, because in trying to be realistic your very mind will revolt and kick against it. In this instance you may need to use survival instinct to fight back. So when this is done, a clearer picture of your business would be revealed to you.

One sure revelation you may get from this exercise is that, you may discover that you are in a wrong business and may need to quit it. But do not despair; you are already in it. Remember; what drove you into that business was profit. Now, having discovered that the business is no longer viable or profitable, what should you do? This time you need to revisit the business plan, not with profit in view but on how the business will work.

The truth to note at this juncture is that, all businesses are profitable, but the profitability of a business is a function of the workability of that business. Consequently, a failed business or one with no profitability is a function of a failed workability. Now, we shift our attention briefly to the man who discovered the electric (incandescent) bulb – Thomas Edison. This great inventor had embarked on a business that kept failing because what prompted him into the business was profitability. Profitability in this regard was that right before he embarked on the research, the result was in view.

So what this great scientist did then was to work from the result. This was the reason for the repeated failure. You would recall that when he finally cracked the puzzle he realized that all the times he failed were the logical process that eventually led to the result.

Most failures we have today are results of inadequate adherence to the process of attainment. Your business failure may be tied to a faulty foundation – faulty business model and preparation. You may need to revisit your beginning to ascertain the overriding factor in your decision to embark on that business. This is because you need not to suffer unduly as a result of a faulty business plan.

4. Faulty Team

If the foundation of your business is rested on a faulty team the death of the business is imminent. I was elated when I read the *Rules of Wealth* by Richard Templar. Here was a man that conquered all odds to get to the top. One lesson I leant from that book was that as much as we can, we must avoid employing family members in our business. That statement can only be credited to a man filled with honesty and sincerity. Do you know that there are very few family businesses that thrive through all odds? Those that do are those whose owners relinquished control of the business to qualified professionals.

What is the composition of your business team? Is your business team made up of your father, mother, brothers, wife, children etc.? If this is the composition of your business, you should be rest assured that your business will fail. Like Richard Templar, in his book, you should be able to fire a defaulting staff without feeling any guilt. Now tell me, how do you fire your father, mother, child or any defaulting relation in your business, without being called up to face a panel, or jury, which of course would be made up of disgruntled relation, that have already found you guilty of the act, long before you appeared before them?

Your ailing business could be a function of your team. Who are your team members? At this point you must realize that a business that dies one or ten years after being set up must have died at inception. What happened in the course of time is just a revelation of the death that had taken place in the past or at inception.

A BUSINESS THAT DIES NOW MAY HAVE JUST REVEALED THE DEATH THAT HAD TAKEN PLACE AT THE INCEPTION OF THE BUSINESS.

Your team should be that comprising people, whose responsibilities are a function of their skills, knowledge and abilities, and, not because they are people who are related to you. The reason for a proper match of duties with capabilities is that, delivery would be thorough, and your business runs orderly and smoothly.

The advice therefore, is that, it is better not to assemble a team at all, than to assemble the wrong team, because assembling a wrong team is like pointing a loaded gun to one's head and pressing the trigger. You already know the outcome – death. So, you do not want to kill your business with your hands, and if you must not, then avoid the killer called "The wrong team".

5.   **"You"**

As we round up on foundational business killers, I wish to state that, I almost skipped this part, because of this very killer – "You or Me".

"You or Me" could be a faulty business foundation. Let's look at Proverb 6:7-11:

"Go to the ant, thou sluggard; consider her ways, and be wise: which having no guide, overseer or ruler, provideth her meat in the summer, and gathereth her food in the harvest.
How long wilt thou sleep, O sluggard? When wilt thou arise out of thy sleep?

YET A LITTLE SLEEP, A LITTLE SLUMBER, A LITTLE FOLDING OF THE HANDS TO SLEEP: SO SHALL THY POVERTY COME AS ONE THAT TRAVELLETH AND THY WANT AS AN ARMED MAN?"

The key words in this passage are '**slumber', 'sleep' and 'poverty'**. The implied meaning of slumber and sleep is laziness, and sleep here implies failure and possible death.

The aforementioned passage refers to most humans and for the purpose of this book, it refers to business owners. It is sad to note that a man who had taken so much time and energy to plan and set up a business would be the same man that uses his own hands to kill the business. You may need to refer to Chapter One (ASSASSIN "YOU"). However, for emphasis, it is needful to point out that a lot of failed businesses today, are a function of failed ownership. A man that spends all his time and resources to set up own-business, but fails to see and keep the business running due to laziness and neglect could be said to have assassinated his business. An inventory of most failed businesses, would reveal that some business owners neglected their businesses and go into slumber. Having spent so much in setting up a business, and probably hiring the best hands to run the business, a business owner may be tempted to hand-over that business to a stranger to oversee.

One thing they failed to realize is that an average man is both selfish and self-centered and may at any cost, take advantage of the opportunities the business offers, to feather his own nest. You know what? A lot of business owners have been relegated to poverty and want, whereas, some of their former employees are thriving in wealth and affluence, having enriched themselves at their expense. This is owing to the negligence of the business owner. Every other month, I come across people, who complain about how their business was almost wrecked because they left the running of their business in the hands of someone else. So you think that you are the only one destined to be rich, you lie and, have failed to take into consideration the selfish and self-centered nature of man.

As true as the above may sound, you are solely responsible for your failure, because you took the decision to go to sleep; leaving your account to another to manage. So while you fold your hands in slumber, someone else is enriching himself at your expense – as a result of your negligence. So you are responsible for your failure and, the killing of your business. Marvel not that the writer of proverbs, in the referenced passage, referred you to the ants. You can imagine the relegation – man is being referred to take a cue from an ant – why the ant, and what lessons are there, to be learnt from the ant?

A Lesson from the Ants

I have decided to dedicate a whole segment to this tiny but wonderful creature – all because, you and I must learn not to kill our businesses with our own hands. Let's recall the quote again.

"GO TO THE ANT, THOU SLUGGARD; CONSIDER HER WAYS, AND BE WISE: WHICH HAVING NO GUIDE, OVERSEER, OR RULER, PROVIDETH HER MEAT IN THE SUMMER, AND GATHERETH HER FOOD IN THE HARVEST"

Apart from humans with varied activities, animals in general, do not face the type of specialized challenges we face – they just live. But because of our make-up, we are daily confronted with different challenges and aspirations; we compete with one another. We strive for fame and glory; we like trends.

Now imagine, if with our intelligence we are still being asked to consult the ant for knowledge, it shows that, a lot needs to be done by man. Let's sail back to the issue at hand.

These tiny creatures are guideless; have no ruler over them and yet one good lesson you need to learn from then as a business owner is that, they work around the clock. That is not to say, they don't rest. They work in and out of season. They provide their meat when it is dry season, because they know that the rainy season is not the best time for them to do that - the flood could sweep them away. So they take time to study the season so as to stay alive by safeguarding their business (that is, finding food to eat).

But you man, that has only set up a business, all you do is to spend from the business repeatedly; stay away from the business; you are always on the move. Tell me, why that business won't die? Because you have failed to provide for the rainy season, so while you are busy squandering, another is gathering from your abandoned labour, no marvel while poverty catches up with you, your subordinates soars in affluence. To this end, you need to note these foundational killers that can ruin not only your business, but completely kill the business.

Chapter Three: The Killer Receptionist

The customers are depleting, have you considered your reception and the front desk officer? Do you know that your receptionist is a reflection of your business? Do you know that the receptionist is as important, if not greater than the CEO or owner of a business?

If you know the aforementioned, happy are you, but if you do not, I wish to inform you that apart from you – the business owner that can decide to suddenly terminate, your business. One very power source that can also suddenly terminate and kill your business is your receptionist. No matter how superfluous your brand is, if this is not reflected by your receptionist, your business is failing and is under threat. A lot of ailing businesses today got infected by their receptionist. Before you proceed further, I wish to narrate two stories - my experience at two different offices. The first was at a government agency (a very powerful agency at that). The second was at a large multinational organization.

Let me start with the former, I had gone to that agency for the first time, or so on invitation. As I approached the building, the simplicity was unique, the surrounding was okay; all about the structure seemed okay, until I came in contact with the receptionist and we began to talk. As the conversation progressed, the receptionist was not looking at me, and when she eventually did, she was frowning. I will try and recall the conversation as best as I can:

Receptionist: "Yes! Who are you? What do you want?" (Sorry what is the problem – either way).

Me: "Good morning madam, I wish to see…."

Receptionist: "Who?" She was speaking overly loud.

Me: "Mr…."

At this point you could feel her resentment, unwillingness at the job she had been assigned to do and also the frown.

Receptionist: "Go upstairs-turn and turn", she had responded. She could not make any attempt to call even with the telephone on the desk.

Me: "Please, be clear on the description", I said.

Receptionist: "That's the best I can do, you can find your way", she had responded with an air of indifference.

I left her desk and wandered through the building, asking questions until I located the office. Guess what I learnt later, the receptionist was not a trained receptionist, but she was only asked to mount the reception desk and feign to be one. For obvious reasons, a lot of people that come to that office may never return to do business with the organization. No thanks to the carefree attitude of the employee at the reception. Till date that incident is still fresh in my mind.

On my second encounter, I met with three receptionists. I would describe them as best as I can, but let me start from the building. The building was a masterpiece. I learnt some millions of dollars were spent on the structure, to reflect what the business stands for. So as I approached the building, I felt a type of serenity; the air was great, neatness was astounding, then I approached the well-crafted receptionists' desk: there were three ladies there. One was sitting, and the others, standing. They were discussing.

These ladies were well dressed, and of course they were pretty too. As I stood before them, I discovered that the receptionist sitting was making-up, while conversing with the one standing. Curiously, I found that they weren't talking in low tones. Interestingly, the third lady was busy chewing gum and none of them bothered to raise their heads, to attend to me, and it didn't matter if I came there for business. Then, without raising their head to look at who just greeted them, the one chewing gum and writing responded.

Receptionist: "Afternoon, how can we help you."

Me: "I wish to see Mr. ..."

Without any further question she handed me a form without looking at me, with an instruction.

Receptionist: "Fill the form. Behind you is the lift. The person you want to see is on the 9th floor (I'm not too sure of the floor)."

All the while, the conversation was ongoing. The other two were engrossed in their conversation, while the one talking to me was busy applying make-up!

Again, like my previous experience, I fumbled through the building, aided by the lift attendant. And with a building as complex as the one I had just visited, it was not impossible to mistakenly enter the toilet, the kitchenette, as well as the escape before being re-directed to my destination.

These two experiences have long been on my mind, and I could not, but wonder how many people have had this kind of experience, and what their response had been. Before I proceed further, I wish to state that the later company has always been bedeviled by series of failures, and instability in terms of structure, ownership and profitability. I wonder if the receptionists and their attitude at the front desk is not a major contributory factor to these problems – problems that had put the company on a lifeline.

Just like I earlier stated, these two institutions mentioned are places I do not pray to visit for any reason, whatsoever. Now imagine the loss of one client or customer, you can also imagine the implication of that loss. This is because, a customer lost is equivalent to the loss of a company's customer, and prospective customers. So, how does a company thrive, when its source of profitability is lost, and the same company must pay the salaries of those who drive its customers away? Remember, the receptionists would always collect their salaries, whether the company is on the path of profitability, or not.

So many businesses have become extinct as a result of the negligence of certain people in its workforce. A lot of companies have failed to see the necessity of training their receptionists, this failure have led to the failures of most organizations. You don't just put anybody to mount your reception; the reason is not far-fetched:

FIRST IMPRESSION LASTS AND IS DIFFICULT TO ERASE

What you should realize is that, no matter how much you have invested in your business, you need to invest much more in your receptionists, because the first impression most people would have of your company starts with them. So, you need to do the following, and note the consequences of not doing them:

1.   Keep Your Reception in Shape

You have said so much about your company in the advertorials; you have portrayed your business to be great; you have also said how orderly your firm is, and how your firm can render one service, or the other. You even claim to be an expert at organizational up-lifting of people, and their life, yet the first thing a client that enters your office sees, is your disorganized reception.

Now, you wonder why a first time visitor never returns, you need to consider the state of your reception. How comfortable are the seats and how serene is your reception? How fresh is the air? Is the air of your reception so foul that, a visitor would feel very uncomfortable?

Mind you, if your reception is so uncomfortable, most clients would be in a haste to leave, and in most cases, would not conclude the business they came for. Do your seats and other furniture fittings portray your company in a light different from what you are, and what you stand for? You need to regularly visit your reception. Take time to seat there, feel the air and ascertain the state of comfort. Then ask yourself: If I were a client, or customer, would I like to stay here longer, or would I wish to come back to this place some other time? In so doing, you have to consider the manager of the area.

2. The Receptionist

I love the author of *Small Business, Big Life* – Luis Barajas. He said in that book that, quite a number of times, he would call his reception to see how the receptionist picks up the phone and responds. Steps like this are very vital if you must escape from the grips of a killer receptionist. You need to upgrade, and know who manages the most important aspect of your business.

You need to know and do the following:

(a) **Train your receptionist:** You don't just put anybody to run your reception - that person must be trained on how to dress, speak, and attend to customers. An ill-dressed receptionist would portray your business as one that is ill and nobody goes to a hospital that is reputed for deaths.

(b) **Monitor his/her words:** Your receptionist needs to know the kind of words to use at the right time. He or she must be told that words like:"What is your problem?" "What do you want?" "Who are you?" and lots more should never be used.

A man visited an office and the first question he was confronted with was: "What is your (the) problem?"

Now you can imagine you visiting an office and being asked this kind of question! Now, what made the receptionist feel the man was there because he had a problem? One thing you must realize is that, even if your firm is a hospital, and you are quite sure that most of the people that would come there have one form of problem or the other, such a question should be well phrased, like:

"Welcome sir (or ma'am). How may we be of assistance to you?"

Your need to also avoid the usage of words that could infuriate your client or customers, like

"How can we help you?"

Nobody wants to be seen as a liability, even if they are, and you don't want them to see themselves in that light. So, as much as you don't want to see your customers sad, and unwilling to return, because of the poor communication of your receptionists, then train them.

(c) **Monitor their dressing:** Your receptionist should be well dressed at all times and must not use the reception desk as a point of make-up, when she could do that at the cloak room, or a more private location.

(d) **Pay the receptionist well:** You need a lively, happy and well dressed person to run your reception and these cannot just be achieved by mere plans, you need to pay the price. In a lot of organization, the receptionists are least paid. This cannot be right. If only the owners know that the receptionist can mar, or make their business! So, what you expect much from, you must be willing to invest much in. You must be ready to position your receptionist such that he/she would be happy and as much as possible, be in the right frame of mind. Money can help you achieve this.

(e)**Select a calm person:** Your reception should not be battle ground. It's a place for calm and organized individuals, because the contrary will portray your organization as restive. A calm and approachable person should run your reception - you need to ensure that issues and things are properly handled.

(f) **Keep it simple:** Finally, you need to keep your reception as much as possible simple, and your receptionist too. He/she does not have to be loud. I have gone to offices where the receptionists are so loud in their appearance. This may sometimes be intimidating to a customer (or client), or may be repulsive, depending on the individual.

You need to create an environment that will keep your client coming, and coming back again. You don't need a seductress as a receptionist. I can bet you that, a lot of people would be turned off, and those that would be turned-on would only come to your office because of your receptionist and not necessarily, because of the service you render.

Now you know. Don't say you have not been told, your business rests not only in your goods and services, processes, operations and you; it also rests in the hands of a prospective killer that must be tamed - **your receptionist(s).**

Chapter Four: The Killer HR

Apart from you and your investment in your business, your human resources management team is very relevant to your business. A thing to note here is that your receptionist is a product of your HR team. If your business is run by a poor HR team, be assured that the death of that business is imminent. So you must ensure that you don't just want to rest the fate of your business on a restive team.

Your HR is responsible for recruiting, and management of the people that run your business. You need to understand that, if you hand over your house to a mad man, that house would be turned to a den of insanity, likewise your business. Your business is a reflection of your HR team.

Your HR team can kill all aspects of your business and this would be done when the wrong set of people are employed to run your business. No wonder, a lot of employers would want to have contact with a new employee, but how many employees can one man see? This would be hectic. Be that as it may, you need a credible team to do that job for you, because if there is one thing that kills business slowly and surely, it is your HR team.

So you need to know your HR team – who and what they stand for, so as to ascertain the calibre of staff they would recruit for your organization.

Characteristics of the Killer HR

(1) Unskilled Personnel:

How did you come about your HR team? If you are not sure of the people manning your HR, you need to stop whatsoever you are doing now and summon that team, because your business rests on them.

Again, is your business ailing? Your first point of call, apart from your product and customer base, should be your HR. The reason being that, your product, customer and how they fair, is a function of the personnel handling them. So, then, the question is: Who is responsible for the hiring? Your HR should be responsible, and responsive enough to do a thorough job of hiring the right staff.

You need to ascertain that those managing your human resources are skillful and well trained to do that job, because if an untrained and unskilled man is asked to recruit and train skilled personnel, you can imagine the kind of product that exercise would yield.

You don't want to leave your well crafted business in the hands of a novice to run. So you need to do all it takes to get the HR personnel, to save your business from collapse, occasioned by the engagement of wrong set of people – that is, if the business is already ailing.

(2) The Corrupt HR:

The world we are in today has become bedeviled with the demand and receipt of gratification. This is not only prevalent amongst law-enforcement agents; it is a sadly so, amongst recruitment personnel. There have been cases, where HR personnel negotiate with prospective employees. They sometimes, demand for the first salary of the employees as gratification, when such employees, eventually sail through the employment hurdle. Now tell me, would such a person be able to make the right selection? One thing you must understand is that a corrupt HR team would, in most cases end up recommending the wrong personnel for different positions in the organization.

The consequences of this kind of attitude are dire. The first is that, a wrong person would assume the wrong position. Secondly, such a person that fails to carry out his duties properly would be left in that same position, because of the process by which such position was secured, and by so doing, things would not work out. Eventually, this engenders inadequacy and failure of the system. So, you wouldn't want to leave your business at the mercy of a corrupt HR. You may need to routinely assess your HR through baits and investigation, to be sure that they are not involved in such killer acts.

(3) They Employ Relatives At All or no Cost:

One good sign of the killer HR is that, they run your business with their family members, friends, relations and acquaintances. Recall what was said in Chapter five under the sub-heading 4: *Faulty team.* There, we did stress the consequence of running your business with family members, as members of staff, and how such could eventually kill your business. Now imagine your business is being run by the family of your HR team, you already know that, to sack a defaulting family member, would place you at the front of a jury that has already found you guilty. So, this could occur in your business. Incidentally, this very trend has killed a lot of businesses.

One thing to note is that, while your business ails these groups of people and their family thrives, because the resources being depleted are yours and not theirs. The consequence of this kind of action is the reason a lot of company would not employ members of the same family. In cases where two people get married a lot of company would recommend that one of the couple should resign.

The question therefore is: Do you take time to examine if a family has not indirectly taken your business? Have you taken time to find out if your ailing business is not a function of your HR's saddling your business with friends and associates, that are not qualified? The truth is that, when a man brings in his friends and associates into a business, he would be beclouded by sentiments and a blurred vision, and this is especially so, when it comes to selection with respect to appropriate skills and qualification.

Is your business ailing? You need to check your employees and their background. Sometimes, the problem could be traceable to your HR.

(4)Wrong Salary Package:

A business, running under a wrong salary package, instituted by your HR is dead and awaiting burial. Whether you know it or not, the moment your salary scheme is inadequate, you are running a dead business, because it will surprise you to know that most of your staff would be with you in body and not in their mind. The consequence of having staffers that are half-hearted is that, their job will be done with little or no commitment. The reason is not far-fetched, for how would you explain a situation where a subordinate earns more than his supervisor.

Apart from the aforementioned, how do you explain an unjust salary scale where the distance between two levels of staffs or a superior and subordinate (or immediate subordinate) is so much, that you would need to convince people that the latter is the deputy. A faulty HR will plunge your business into this evil, and the moment your business operates at that level, it has not only been killed, it is at the burial stage.

(5) Inattentive:

The killer HR is one that is inattentive, careless and would not listen to the cries and complaints of members of staff. So, while members of staff are groaning, and the HR fails to manage the situation, the organization ends up with aggrieved personnel doing their job half-heartedly, with a focus to exit the job at the slightest opportunity.

Like earlier mentioned, when members of staff are working under an inadequate salary system and under an insensitive HR, they may leave the company without necessarily notifying management.

Now, you may need to understand the consequences of an un-notified exit. The fact remains that, no matter how soon you get a replacement, there is always a loss. In most cases, the cost of upgrading a new staff is much more than the cost of retention of an old staff. If your HR is not sensitive to your staff, they will, by default, bring your business to a sudden end. So, be very sure of what your HR is doing, in terms of staff welfare.

One thing you need to understand is this: When a business (let's assume it is a thriving business) is under the death spell of an HR, the business' gradual death may not be so obvious, but one thing that is certain is this, that business is on a lifeline, and when its destruction comes, it will be sudden and it will take the owners by surprise.

So, your thriving business may actually be ailing and dying without your notice; even though, the signs may not be obvious, some traits could still be seen. These include:

1) The sudden exit of staff from your organization – particularly old and competent hands.
2) Unskilled staff running your business (failure and litigation are pointers to this).
3) Complaints and threats; if you keep your ears on the ground.

A lot would be there for you to see, but if you are that careless and carefree entrepreneur, your eyes would be shut to these. The warning therefore, is that you should not only be at alert, but must open your eyes, as a lot of examples of business that were killed by the HR are all around us. So, you can decide to rescue your business, or allow it to go down, but mind you it is your business and its drowning will drag you along.

Chapter Five: Save Your Business from the Killer C.M.S.

There are two very vital components of a business, these are the customers (or clients) and profitability. A business that lacks these two things has failed. So, before you go any further, you need to know this fact – that you need not dissipate much effort to protect your business than you need to protect your customers.

YOUR CUSTOMERS ARE MORE IMPORTANT THAN YOUR BUSINESS – YOU   NEED TO PROTECT THEM.

Your customers must be protected and not your business, because your business existence is purely dependent on the existence of your customers. I believe you already know this, that the more success you have with your customers, the more the upgrade of your business and of course, profitability. This same position is true, for non-profit organizations. The truth is that, the profit of that organization is the attainment of customers (no matter who these may be – all businesses have one form of clients, or customers) satisfaction. The more this satisfaction is met, the more successful such organization becomes.

Your clients, customers and profits are so relevant to your business, and you need to protect them. That means, you need to focus more on those members of staff that interact more with these people in your business. They are what I classify, as C. M. S – there are killers in this group that must be tamed. **C.M.S here refers to customer care, marketers and sales representatives.** Hope your business is not being run by a killer customer care personnel, marketers, or sales representative? If you are not sure of the answer to that query, here is how to identify their operations.

1. The Killer Customer Care

Recall, your business success is dependent on your customer's satisfaction, not on your products quality control. Your product would be worthless, if the end-user is not satisfied with it. Assuming, you have a defaulting product that has failed to satisfy your customers, does that mean that is the end of your business? Of course not! This is the reason why most businesses have the customer care unit – a unit that is meant to cater and appease the aggrieved customer.

I wish to restate that the main focus of the customer care unit is to attend to new or old customers. Its core duty and responsibility is to cater for the customers at all cost, so as to appease the customer and consequently win the customer to your business. And that must be done irrespective of the status of your product.

Mind you, a good product or service must be presented to the customer in a perfect form. In as much as this is so, I want you to realize that even with a sub-standard product, a good customer care team, should be able to retain your customers forever. That team, should be able to create a lasting impression on the mind of an aggrieved customer, to the extent that the customer would be willing to come back again – if not for the poor product, but with the hope of getting a good product. Your customer care team can create and recreate that situation. Alas, what do we have scattered all over the world? Most businesses today have a group of personnel manning the customer care unit with little or no interest in the progress and growth of the business.

Let's delve deep into this very serious and important issue, with reference to a period in the banking industry in Nigeria – a period that span between the 80s to probably the late 90s and beyond. The memory of most Nigerians, as far as the banking sector is concerned, is still very fresh. As young as I was then, I hated the concept of visiting a bank – the reason was not far-fetched. Apart from the long queues that characterized the banking halls during those periods, the customers almost always left the banks sad, after cashing their money, not because of the hours spent in the bank, but because of the banking officials – especially the customer care personnel.

In those days most of the banks that operated then, were like demi-gods, and they frequently assumed the position of supremacy. Customers were not so important to them. They felt they had enough and as such the customers were often faced with unfriendly remarks such as:

"If you can't wait, you can leave. A lot of people are there waiting"

"We don't need your money: be fast I have a lot to do, I did not leave my house to attend to you alone"

The list is endless. A lot of customers, those days, were aggrieved, but they had no choice than to stick to such banks even till date, with a clause I will explain much later.

An important fact, I wish to bring to your notice is that, decades after the banking revolution in Nigeria, which saw the emergence of new banks, what transpired then still annoy most Nigerians, save those that didn't experienced that period. Till date you find people still talking about that period with so much annoyance and hatred. To crown it all, almost all of those banks that treated their customers that way, have only succeeded in retaining their customers account, and not the customers. If you are privileged to meet someone with an account in such bank, they will tell you that they rarely go to such bank for any transaction; their preference has been bought over by the new generation banks.

Now if the aforementioned is true, your guess is as good as mine. Quite a number of the banks, excluding those that have embraced change, had to contend with massive loss of customers and the consequences – you already know. As earlier stated, some of these banks were smart enough to combat this evil and they quickly worked on their customer care unit. No marvel then, that, one of such banks drives the Nigeria banking sector.

Mine is not to analyze the banking industry in Nigeria, but to draw attention to the consequences of allowing your business to be ruined by a faulty customer care unit. This is guaranteed to bring your business to a sudden end, no matter your investment in that business.

Let's tackle some of the traits of the killer customer care unit:

Traits of the Killer Customer Care
(a) Poor Attitude:

What a customer, or client needs most from your business is "attitude". But what do we have today? When a customer manages to scale through the receptionist, hoping to receive desired results, they are confronted with a "disgusting "customer care representative.

How can you imagine a customer that is kept waiting endlessly instead of being attended to by a customer care representative, who is busy chatting with others in the presence of the customer, and when the customer makes attempt to draw his, or her attention, they are waved down, as if to ask him to exercise more patience. An attitude of this kind would possibly make your client, or customers discard your product – with, or without a substitute.

(b) The Scary Gaze:

Nobody likes to be looked down upon, or frightened by the look on another's face. Have you, or did you take out time to examine that person you've chosen to run your customer care, and how he looks at people? If you have a high minded fellow with a bad gaze to man that position, most customers that come through the front door would leave through the back door, and may never return.

(c) Unfriendly Words:

Words they say: "Once spoken can never be retrieved", even though retracted. You cannot erase it from the memory of the hearer. Till date I still remember some of the ill words spoken to me. You may have forgotten the fight you had with someone in the past, but how often are our days spoilt, when we remember some of the ill words spoken against us. Sometimes you even wished you never came in contact with such a person.

So, it is when, instead of attending to a customer with friendly words, a customer care representative makes repulsive and offensive statements. Some of these customer care representative do not see anything bad in screaming at their customers. Of course, the business is not theirs, so, they are careless about what happens to the business. But remember the business is yours and so, it would be unwise for you to sit and fold your hands, while someone, or a group of people ruin your business.

(d) The War of Words:

It grieves my heart, when I enter an office and discover that the customer care people are busy arguing with clients and customers, instead of attending to them. Many companies have tried to display the sign that reads: "The customer is always right" on their wall but it ends there. What you find in most businesses today are "war of words" going on with the customer, who intends to seek for the solution to a product, or services that has failed to meet his expectations. Why wouldn't there be argument, when your customer care uses words like: "Are you sure you can read, or are you sure you read the manual THOROUGHLY?"

Were you there when the person read through the manual? So what makes you feel that process was not done thoroughly? And even if you are sure it was not done thoroughly, who made you the judge? Yours is to attend to the customer and not to unnecessarily interrogate him - HELP HIM.

"Look here, don't teach me my job!" Or, "You can't teach me my job!"

How would a customer not try to teach you your job, when, instead of listening and attending to him, you argue? What you must realize at this juncture is that no serious minded person would want to go to an office if all he expects is argument.

Your customer care representative must learn words control, and should be made to know that the customer must not be subjected to argument, instead they should be listened to, as well as respected.

(e) **The Contending Personnel:**

There are cases of customer care representatives, fighting with customers. This should not be mentioned in your business, as this portends sudden death of that business. Your customer has a right of expression that does not necessarily, need to tally with your belief. Remember also, that your customer is your customer, and must be carefully handled and, not mistreated.

When you fight with one customer, you lose several customers. The reason is not far-fetched. The customer, being a rational being, would think within himself that, if the purchase or use of a product means combat, then, it is better to look elsewhere. That would be the decision of customers, after having experienced such a lackluster confrontations.

2. The Killer Marketer
A lady recently told me that her company policy of just taking anybody that agrees to market their products have become more

stringent. She said that, such an applicant will not only be orally interviewed; such an applicant would have to write aptitude test, and of course other things would follow. When I analyzed her story, I realized what the company has come to term with:

A WRONG MARKETER CANNOT BE DIFFERENT FROM THE PRODUCT- A WRONG PRODUCT.

The company must have realized that, the image it projects is a function of the marketers` interface with the public. Assuming they had the right product, and a wrong person, with little, or no information to market the product, you can guess the outcome – failure.

Getting a customer is one thing, how you go about getting that customer is another thing. Selling a product is one thing, how you go about selling that product is another. But in most cases, how do you go about this process – your marketer(s). You need not think too far. If your marketers have failed to up you outcome through sales, you probably have the wrong team marketing the right product, so you need to rescue your business before the string on which it is hanging and dangling breaks.

Traits of the Killer Marketers

(a) I Don't Know:

Watch out for anybody that is fond of using this slogan, such a person is a killer marketer and must not be found with your product.

How does one sell a product that he or she knows little or nothing about? It is like running a business one has no knowledge about. So it is, when the person marketing your product and services lacks adequate knowledge of what the products and services they are marketing is all about. They should be trained, not to display ignorance to the customer, rather they should use the phrase: "Let me get back to you with more details", instead of "I don't know". Please note, that an "I don't know" marketer will cost you the life of your business, because that business would be starved of customers.

(b) Poor Out-Look

There is a popular mantra that, "A man is a reflection of his companion and not necessarily what he sees of himself in the mirror". That is quite true. As far as marketing is concerned, you may not be there, but there is someone marketing your products and services, and if this person is shabby, dull and unassuming, it is difficult to see how this will help your business. It is doubtful, if people will be willing to embrace your products or services.

Over the years, I have seen a lot of companies fail to pay their marketers and would rather put them on commission. Fine, there is nothing wrong in placing a staff on commission, but you need to know that the person may be a fresh graduate, or one that has serious financial challenge. Now, you want this person to market your well designed product in his poverty-stricken state. How does he get the attention of the intended client, or customer, if he or she looks shabby? So you need to empower that person with an initial fund to upgrade his/her appearance and outlook. The initial cost may be much in the short run, but the gains in the long run, is inexhaustible. You would be amazed at how much such a person would bring into your business by his marketing runs.

Do you still wonder why your marketers are not performing? You need to consider upgrading their outlook. Fine you may put them on commission, but they need to look well, to do well and attract quality customers.

(c) Lack of Confidence

It is doubtful whether many a marketer would be able to field some forms of questions, especially if they have no confidence in themselves. Sometimes, a simple question such as, "Yes from where?" could see a fidgeting marketer, blank out. Does this describe your marketer? A good marketer is one that can sell ice to an Eskimo, and one way that could be effective is an unabated confidence. You know what confidence is – the assurance of something. True, but to a good marketer, confidence is the assurance of everything. When you have an all-knowing marketer, that is easily frightened by a little tilt, the customer, yet to be captured, will flee.

I know a very seasoned marketer, though not very fluent, yet passionate and confident about the products she markets. She speaks, in very confident manner, about the products she markets, including things, which are not part of the products, in a way and manner that before you know it, you have issued her a cheque. How awful it could be when your marketer, despite all the training and investment, isn't bold in defending your products, or services due to the lack of confidence! While your products, or services are very important, the carrier of such services/products, must note that, with confidence, even the man that does not need the product, might be carried away.

To emphasize what confidence can do to a product, I wish to illustrate, using the encounter between a seasoned preacher to an unwilling mind. That preacher was Paul the Apostle, and the unwilling mind was Governor Felix, a renowned Roman Governor. This was a Governor that resented Christianity, being confronted by Paul, who, as at the time of Governor Felix's contact with him, had been converted to the Christian faith. The confidence with which Paul talked of Christ and Christianity to Felix was so much that his unwillingness to accept the religion was completely broken and he trembled and declared:

"Go thy way for this time, when I have a convenient season, I will call for thee."

(Acts 24:25).

This is what knowledge, coupled with confidence, can do when you market a product. The intending customer may not respond immediately, but there will be a recall at a convenient time.

(d) Lack of Interest

What drives your marketer? If it is not interest, try to arouse interest in him, and if it cannot be aroused, such a person should not be in your team. An uninterested marketer is like a horse been forced to drink water from a stream. What a futile effort that would be! Unfortunately unemployment has forced a lot of people into the job of marketing. No wonder, why, even with so many marketers, customers are still elusive.

So, you need to be very specific in the recruitment process. The interest of the intending marketer must be ascertained, and this is especially so, if the applicant is not a marketer by training. It must be noted that, even though such an applicant is not a marketer by training; with interest, excellence is guaranteed. You also have a role to play in arousing the interest of the person marketing your product or services with the provisions of incentives. Please note that a solid reward system would enhance this process and create and arouse his interest.

3. The Killer Sales Representative

The customer care, the marketer and the product points to one direction – the customers and his satisfaction. While the marketers bring in the customers, the sales representatives make available the products to the customers. While the customers care representatives' duty is to keep the customer satisfied, and also to remain with the organization.

Products must be sold and people are responsible for the products' sale. At one end of this process, are the company's representatives (the sales representatives), while at the other end, are the end users (customers or clients). One thing is certain and that is, organization or business must have been set up, with not only the hope of creating the product, but with an intention of selling the product to the consuming public. Thus, thorough consideration must have been given to the consumers. So, then the product is a reflection of their needs. It may either be in goods, or in services. Whatever the case may be, there is a target, and that target must not only gain access to that product; that target must be satisfied.

With all the attributes honey has, one unique characteristic it has is its sweet taste. But do you know that as sweet as honey is, its packaging could make it loose its taste? In addition, the person that handles, or delivers it, could also render that superb taste worthless to the end user. So also, are the killer sales personnel? They could turn a wonderful product into one resented by the customers, for which it is made.

If you analyze this title very well, something would puzzle you and that is the "representative" part of it. The one chosen to represent another, is just like a replica, so, your sales representatives are not just representing themselves; they are brand ambassadors representing both you and of course, your products! How well, these are represented, have their advantages and disadvantages. Bad representation would drag a business to its lowest ebb, if not curtailed. Mind you, your aim here is to identify attribute that makes a sales representative a business killer. Let's look at some of the killer attributes.

Attributes of the Killer Sales Representative

(a) Lack of Representation

Your sales representatives are to represent your business and reflect your products. How sad then, it is, to note that, a lot of the so-called sales representatives have failed to represent the brands, for which they have been assigned. How do you imagine a sales representative that castigates a product he, or she is meant to project the same to the customers?

"Well, I just sell this product. I don't use it; neither do I believe in it. One must survive and anything that avails itself of survival must be embraced – here I am".

A lot of sales representative either say the above, or behave it. Now, how do you convince a buyer with attitudes that depicts the non-workability, or inadequacy of a product? Of course, the product is not well represented and if this is the case, the sales would be impaired.

Representation could come in any form. You have just seen one that is utterance-based. That also could be reflective of the behaviour of a so-called representative. The sales representative out-look also matters. For how do you explain a shabbily dressed sales representative of a superb fashion outfit? Such a person would portray that outfit in an ill manner because a typical customer would rather assess your product first, with the person that represents your products. You may have the best of fashion design, but if your sales representative lacks that fashion sense, be very sure that a lot of customers would spend far less time, surveying and probably purchasing your products. You need to be very sure that the person chosen to be your sales representative has the winning attributes. Be sure that, the one that would represent your products has both the appearance and the charisma, so as to bring about results that exceed your expectation. That person must be well packaged to properly represent your products.

The sad truth today is that a lot of sales representatives are actually business killers, for failure to *properly* represent the products they sell! When you deal with people that do not properly represent your products as they should, your business is heading for the rocks.

(b) Sales Without Customer:

I have seen companies saddle their sales representatives with unrealistic targets, without taking into consideration, due modalities and the realities on ground. Fine, you have the products and your investment are tied to it, but what you must realize is that if your target is to sell your product at all cost and by any means, you may end up setting up a team that will sell your products, while your customer base depletes!

Here, you find some sales representatives, purchasing the products themselves and because these purchases are target-driven, such products may be forced on a customer that does not really need the product! The result of these types of sales may initially be on the positive side, but overtime, the outcome will manifest, as diminishing returns.

Here, is how it reflects: The sales representative may initially look successful, but mind you, such purchase is usually tied to a fixed income. In most cases, the person may have managed to exceed the limit at the initial stage, but as time goes on, a state of equilibrium would be attained, where sales become stagnant.

The sad truth is that, at this stage of stagnancy, it becomes clear that the sales was not borne out of the existence of a true customer base, thus, the law of diminishing returns would then, set in. Again, this is because, most of the customers that have the products, which were somehow forced on them, may still have quite a lot of them in their custody. And assuming, they are retailers, they may not be willing to accept more of that product. What happens here is that, you cannot succeed at the sale of a product you do not believe in, but since, such client were probably induced into getting such product, a lot may end up, abandoning the product because their investments were induced. The outcome is that, you see such business owners start sacking, shuffling and overhauling their sales team. How sad to note that, this process may just be too late because the business does not actually have, in clear term, a real customer-base. Consequently, such a business starts struggling, profits begin to dwindle, losses are declared, and before you know it, bankruptcy is declared – the business is eventually killed!

(c) Unrealistic Targets:

This is more, or less related to the aforementioned – sales without customer-base. When you run a business without taking out time to do a thorough analysis and preparation before setting up your sales and marketing team, you may be highly misled by your drive, and ultimately, the outcome of such ill drive will be the assemblage of a team, I choose to call "intruders" or "killers". When your business is driven by unrealistic sales targets and timelines, you end up with crooks that would lift up your business to a height and would abandon it at that height. You know what will happen? The business will experience a free fall and its fatality would be terrible, and the impact may be beyond repairs.

Why the hurry, if you have the product and you want the sales? Let the product create the pull and if it does not, then that means you have the wrong product! This is not to discredit the fact that a good product would sell itself, without the right personnel. A good product would naturally sell itself, but you have assembled a sales team to stimulate and enhance the sales, and if that be the case, then that team should not be given a "blind date". They must be sure of the "date" and they must also be made to know that the date they have been given, is just one out of a thousand. So, they must be made to look out for the other "date". This should be their driving force.

"Catch that other date as you did the previous".

When your sales team is so motivated, the need for setting unrealistic target would not arise, instead you would have set their drive in motion. What a lot of business owners fail to do, is to focus on the sales target, instead of the sales drive; the latter would give a greater and lasting success, than the former.

Is your business ailing and you are lost on the direction your sale is headed? You need to examine the *modus operandi* on which targets are set. After this, you need to concentrate on setting sales drive. This is more like motivation for your team. It's just what a good football coach would do to his team. Rather than setting unrealistic targets, a good coach would rather focus on the drive of his team. A well driven team is one that is motivated, and that would propel itself towards attaining the best result possible. On the other hand, a team that is saddled with unrealistic targets without motivation would lose and fail.

You don't want to create a team that is just target driven, but you need a team that is drive- driven; a motivated team; a team that represents the team. When you have this type of team your aim of setting up the business would be achieved and before you know it, your business would be propelled to a height that would sustain itself. So rather than setting unrealistic target, focus instead, on putting a mechanism in motion that, would enhance the drive of your sales team. The result is that, the team would end up; setting a target and meeting that target that exceeds your imagination. You may end up being the one asking them to soft pedal, because success at times, comes with fear, especially when it exceeds ones expectations and aspirations.

(d) Sellers Or Helpers:

Examine your sales representatives; are they sellers, or helpers? A good number of businesses would rather assemble a great number of sellers in the sales team, with a view to selling the company's products. Members of the team on the other hand, have just one thing in view, and that is to sell the company's product, regardless of whether the customer is pleased or not. Their focus is the company, and its product. In other words, their target is to sell the product, so as to please the company.

This concept of pleasing the company at the expense of everything else has never done well for any business in the long run, because such gains cannot be sustained with such flawed habit. The proper order is that, the customers come before the product. The products are for the customer and not otherwise. This implies that, when you focus more on the product, forgetting the customers, you will run at a loss, and that business will eventually die.

What is the make-up of your sales team, are they sellers or helpers? This question is very crucial when you consider Patrick Forsyth's definition of selling in his book *How to Write Report and Proposals*:

"Selling is helping people to buy".

The most important phrase in that definition is 'helping people'. The 'people' stands for customers or prospective customers. So, when you assemble a team that sees themselves, as more of sellers than helpers, they lose sight of the concept of sales and such, may not aid the customers in that, they may not get the right treatment, or aid that, would make them come back for more.

A good sales person is one that goes out to assist the customers, meet his need, and not necessarily, one that sells the product to the customer. The difference between the former and the latter is that, while the former strives for customer's satisfaction, the latter is more concerned with selling the product, with little or no consideration as regards the customer's satisfaction.

Is your business ailing? If you think so, then, consider the attributes of these killers – C.M.S. The problem might be with them, you need to save your business from being killed by these killers.

Chapter Six: Financial Predators

No man in his right senses would place a known thief, as the overseer of his finances and business.

At this stage, I wish to state that I am not too comfortable with the title of this chapter. Apart from the fact that it sounds so unwholesome, it looks uncivil and unethical. I feel I should just remodel it, but something within me tells me that, a thief has only one name and that name, is "thief". So you will bear with me as I am not permitted to alter the name of anyone. Such requires legal backing. And as such, for the purpose of those concerned let's leave that title as it is – financial predators (a thief).

A thief is that person that takes what does not belong to him. It may be done openly or secretly, forcibly or deceitfully, to the knowledge of the owner or otherwise. The fact is, what has been taken was taken without the reasonable, or unreasonable consent of the owner. Some people see their act of stealing as being tactical or smart; some may conceal these acts with their eloquence or educational qualification (degrees). A lot of people may feel that as long as no weapon was involved in the act- that ignoble title should not be assigned to them. One sure fact is that, nobody would assign such title to such a person unless the person is caught; such a person is a thief.

Characteristics of a Thief

1) They are humans.
2) They may be either literate, or illiterate.
3) They may be from any race, belief or religion.
4) They may be neatly dressed, or poorly dressed.
5) They live their lives targeting things that belong to others.
6) They deceive people into the wrong investment.

7)   They steal from their client's portfolio.

8)   They pry on the innocent and play on their intelligence

9)   They falsify figures

10) They encourage others to behave like them.

If these characteristics are found in any one, such a person should be seen in that light. So, may we now go around investigating and looking for people with such characteristics, so that, we may avoid them? Sad to note that, trying to know if someone is so depicted, is like trying to know the thought in a man's heart. Therefore, the likelihood is that, as a business owner you may end up employing such people to run your business. You may also end up putting them in charge of your finances and financial matters. They may be your financial advisers! So if you place a thief to guide your money, you already know the outcome. I hear people say your finances become secured because they would not want to steal it. Yes of course they would not steal that money; they will protect it, so much that at the point, or instance you need the money, what you give them to oversee would be different from what may be handed over to you.

Get this fact very clear, in the business world, thieves don't just take your money and disappear. No! They take your money and disable you. It does not matter, if you arrest, or imprison them, one thing is sure to happen, which is that your business would have been wrecked.

In recent times there have been series of financial fraud, embarked upon by men whom the world at one point or the other saw, as great investors. These people kept on rolling out profits and posting dividends. They completely fooled the world, but at the point their financial records were opened it was discovered that, what was given them, to manage had been completely depleted. The extent of fraud was so much that many have been imprisoned.

Some of these acts have plunged not only some individuals into financial mess, but have dragged the world into the present global frenzy and economic meltdown. A lot of countries are yet to recover from some of these dastardly acts, perpetuated by some of the world's renowned financial gurus, whom, while investors were not keenly watching, were busy squandering their investments.

So, how do you save your business from predators of this nature, or rather, how do you detect them, since as earlier stated, most of them are well camouflaged? They are, of course, always very cute. They seem to know more of financial matters than anybody – including you. Besides, if you need to know them, you can catch them by being watchful. Let's examine some of the traits of these financial predators.

Characteristics of Financial Predators

(1) Knowing All Yet Ignorant of Financial Management:

Is your financial team faring well? Or better still, how is your accountant's performance? Is he so bright financially but lacks the know-how on how to manage your finances? He may be good at taking down records and making payments, yet all or most of the advices he had given in the past have resulted in a loss to the business. If the man handling your finances is so depicted, you have a killer trailing, not only your business, but your very self! Death is imminent.

You need to realize that no matter how perfect your financial records are, if all that results, are losses, your business is worse off; compared to one that does not have financial records. You need to be very sure that your financial advisers are competent, as far as financial management is concerned, or else what you would have, are predators. They are predators, in the sense that, they may not steal from you, but their incompetence would lead you continually, into losses. Their wrong advise, would always amount to financial accidents. And, of course, you are sure; they would keep adequate records of the accidents! You need to ask yourself, whether you set up your business to repeatedly run into financial accidents, or profitability.

Examine your financial team, place them side by side with their outcomes, preceding most of the advice given, this will help you ascertain, if you have financial predators, manning your finances.

(2) Undue Delay of Payments:

Some say that accountants don't like releasing money, which might appear to be typical of them, but if this delay is borne out of ill-intentions, you have a financial predator handling your finances. Consider this instance: A man has done his job, the job has been certified okay by the team of experts responsible for that process, and those that certified the job satisfactory, have also advised that his money be paid. But alas! Undue delays surfaces, when he gets to the finance department. He is pushed from one desk to another. Appointments are scheduled and re-scheduled, because he must be frustrated and compelled to part with some money, from what he is to be paid!

Is your business ailing? If it is, have you tried to find out why most of your customers and partners are not willing to do business with you?

These people may not directly complain to you, but one thing is certain – they may consider that doing business with your organization is not a healthy choice. They may continue with you for some time, but one thing is certain – at the slightest opportunity, they would be forced to abandon you! Be rest assured that they will abandon you, and that, may happen at a time you think you have them as your permanent clients or customers, and you probably need their loyalty. Don't be deceived; you may think that they are dispensable and that you may not find it difficult to replace them. You may have even, forgotten how words (even, those secretly spoken in your closet) were carried by winds to the open.

The implications of this are dire. You have a project; you want people to execute it for you. You are even ready to pay the fees, but dealing with your financial team scares them away. So, what happens to that business? Of course, it is heading for the rocks!

Quite a lot of businesses have had life sniffed out of them because of situations like this, and those responsible for it are left to run and oversee the business! You must remember, however, that those affected, would not speak of your accounts department, when telling others, but rather, they would refer to you and your business, as one not worthy of honest business association, or dealings.

(3) Figure Falsification:

I love how the Oxford dictionary defines the word: "falsify". It defines it as follows: "to alter fraudulently; misrepresent". If your financial team is an embodiment of very smart people, who are good at altering figures fraudulently, then you are running a business, where you lose 90% for 10%; in that, the smart people can short-change you by altering figure from 10 to 100. I would advise you start looking for the very 'dull' personnel, because these smart people would suddenly bring your business to an end.

One good trait of this group of people is that they so easily walk, or talk themselves into the hearts of business owners. They make themselves so diligent and trustworthy, that while the business owners are busy trusting and believing in them, they create reasonable space with which, to trick you into signing cheques that rip off the fortunes of the business.

These kinds of people are very friendly to the CEO. To catch them, you need to be wary of any financial expert, who, instead of concerning himself with what brought him to your office, would first and foremost flatter you and show concern on some personal matters. And while you are busy talking, papers are presented to you to sign. If you are not vigilant, you would find that you have signed off your well crafted business! By the time you realize it, it may be too late. Your creditors may be right beside you asking for liquidation of the business.

I feel very sad seeing business owners, rather than busy running their businesses, are hopping from court to court, trying to prosecute those they have put in charge of their finances. Very few are lucky to recover their money and may only be consoled by the sentencing of such financial predators. But a lot may never recover from the shock of what happened. The reason is not far-fetched. A lot of people put those they trust to run their finances. This would bring me to a story told me by a man I gave a lift, sometime ago.

His friend had a printing press and was doing very well, until he decided to expose himself – family members were those running the business. And of course, these were people he spent much time with, and so he trusted them. Documents were probably signed, without him thoroughly going through them. Blank cheques, in most cases, would have been signed, but guess what happened to that business? All that is left is a dejected man and his travail. Those he brought to run the business enriched themselves at his own expense. You know as much as I do, that a man whose desire was to assist his family would not want to be seen arresting, or having them arraigned before a court of law.

What killed his business? He had family members as financial predators, handling his finances, and they eventually brought the business to a sudden halt.

The advice therefore, is, do not leave your cheque (I mean signed cheque with too many blank spaces), take time to read any document before appending your signature. Above all, do not retain a staff that has been found to have falsified figures. Remember that, it takes one bad egg to spoil the lot.

Chapter Seven: The Killer Packaging and Price-Tag

Your ailing business could be a function of the proposals, or letters leaving your office. It could even be the letter-head papers. Are there mistakes – either typographical, or colour spills? Or, could it be that, the letter head papers are rumpled? These are some of the things you need to consider before sending out letters to clients. Remember, you may not be there, when the letter is being read, but one thing is sure – the letter represents everything about your business. What you should realize is that, any mail from your business is your business ambassador, because it represents you, and how people should perceive you.

You may need to consider the quality of the paper, the logo and the composition represented on the paper. The reason for this is that, in every genuine business, there is an exchange of correspondence, and the response received, is a reflection of how the process is embarked upon.

If you examine your business thoroughly, you would realize that a lot have been written on the foundation of the business – the article of association, application for business name registration, and memorandum of understanding. The list is endless. But then, after these foundational stages, you may advertise through the media or assemble promoters to push your product and services in the marketplace. Assuming all these things have been properly put in place, the turning point would be the turning up of customers. Again, beyond individuals, some of your customers may be corporate organizations. If it is so, correspondences would have been exchanged from time to time. How then, do you handle your correspondences and the materials that convey them?

Do you handle the materials that carry your massages like reports and proposals, as well as, you would handle the information they carry? You may have read all about how to write the best proposal, or report; maybe you have the best literary hands, and your confidence in them is high. But mind you, even with the best brains at your disposal, if the worst material, e.g. letter head paper is used, the output would be poor. The reason for that may not be unconnected with your documents, and its packaging. Document packaging is as important, as their contents.

An easy way out is to observe your reaction, when you receive an envelope or a document addressed to you. By merely looking at an envelope, you could guess the content. We naturally would want to quickly look at what is inside a well packaged envelope, or document, and would not hesitate to put aside, or completely discard one that is not well packaged. In so doing, a lot of very vital information may be lost. Thank God that we are in this era of emails, where most transactions are done online. But the fact is that, the traditional mail cannot be totally replaced by online transactions. A lot of dealings are still being done the traditional way, and a lot of such deals encapsulated in proposals, are being discarded because of wrong packaging.

At this juncture, there is need to let you into how a proposal, or letter from your business could kill your business. Or it may be that you may need to look at them as the root cause of your ailing business. Your customers are depleting, your proposals are not been responded to, you may need to check your letter head paper and the quality of the material used for their printing. You may have a killer not only trailing you, but one that carries your business with it. Know them now!

Characteristics of the Killer Proposal or Letter

This segment has little, or nothing to do with the content of the material leaving your office, but rather, the state of the carrier of the content.

(1) Stains:

You have drafted the letter and proposal all day, and now, it is time to package it. The only choice is a stained letter head paper. What comes to your mind? "Well it does not matter, my friend is at the helm of affairs, we have already concluded on the transaction", you may be tempted to shrug it off. So you send it out that way, and the first person that handles it, sees a terrible letter head paper. Guess what may come to his mind:

"One of these unserious people again".

Guess again, what he may do. Of course, you need not guess too far! The likelihood of that letter being read is slim and if it is ever read at all, it is quite likely, that the content may not be taken seriously. What has happened here is that, a well crafted proposal, with high prospect, has been killed by a poorly packaged material. What is being discussed here is that, you have used a letter head paper, that is, not commensurate with the status of your business. That is to say, the stain on the letter head paper has invalidated it. A stained letter head paper is often discarded! Please, note that, your letter head paper must be stain-free, because a stained letter head paper would do your business much harm, than good.

(2) The Crumpled Paper:

It is very easy to analyze a job applicant that applies for a job using a rumpled paper. We are quick to get such off our list of interviewees, but we also fail to realize that, similar treatment awaits us, when the letters, proposals, or reports that leave our office are crumpled!

The first impression created by a crumpled paper, is un-seriousness, and no serious minded company would want to do business with one seen in that light. Do you know that a little fold or squeeze could portray your business as un-serious, and then if most of the documents that leave your office are crumpled, your business is trailing the path of death? This is because, if the impression created by your outgoing mails is that, your business is not a serious one, you would lose some, if not all, of your prospective customers. What those crumpled letters, or proposals have done to your business, is to retard it. Eventually, that business will die.

Is your business ailing, you may need to examine those documents, you have sent out in the past, if they are crumpled and do the necessary adjustments.

(3) The Broken Bag:

I entered a major IT firm recently to purchase a cartridge for my printer. The customer care personnel handed to me, the cartridge, without packaging it. I guess she felt that, since it was small, that I could handle it. But I insisted that it must be packaged.

"Sorry we don't have any package that size", she insisted.

"So what do you want me to do?" I queried.

Out of resentment, she went through her shelf and handed me a bag. Guess what; one of the handle was broken!

"What is this"? I exclaimed in resentment.

Lo and behold, it transpired that, most of what she had in stock, had one hand each, so I had no choice than, to make do with the bag as it was, with a resolution, never to visit that shop again!

You may be losing lots and lots of customers, not because of your product, but because of your packaging. One thing you must realize is that, a lot of your customers may not necessarily patronize you because of your product, but the outlook of the product and the final packaging may be the magic. So, you need to take adequate notice of how goods purchased from your business are packaged, lest, you would have lots of displeased customers, leaving your store and vowing in their hearts, never to return again – just like my good self.

The Guide/ Check List

There are lots and lots of materials that you may be using to do your business, and yet they are likely impacting negatively, on the success of your business. What I have done, is to give you a sample of the consequences of using a faulty material to do your business.

Here are some sample materials, a lot of businesses use in transactions. Good as they may seem, yet a lot of them, often kill businesses because of how poorly they are used, or presented. You may need to start reexamining some of these things, with respect to your business.

(1) Receipts
(2) Envelops
(3) Delivering notes
(4) Cellophanes
(5) Paper bag
(6) Stamps with ink
(7) Price tag.

These are some of the materials a lot of businesses use. What I want you to realize is that while you lay much emphasis on your

108

products, the materials you use in selling, or delivering these products matter a lot. You may wonder why I said so. This is because a lot of people may not have access to your packaging; however, one thing you must realize is that, your packaging is a good source of advertising your products and services, and that could be an avenue to attract existing, or new customers. If not well handled, it may repel both.

In the business world of today your packaging may not be in the form of a carton or receipt, your packaging may be your letter head paper. Your packaging also includes the paper bags, used in packaging a purchased product.

I know someone who would travel a long journey to make purchases in a retail store, just because of the love he has for their packaging. I know another person who would rather purchase a book at a higher rate in another store, in preference to a store nearby all because of their faulty price tags!

One thing I realized about the latter is that, their price tag is so faulty and it is not customer friendly at all. This is because while there are price tags on the products on the shelves, you may still have to call for assistance at every instance, to ascertain if what you think is the price is correct.

Chapter Eight: The Killer "Tongues of Fire"

We are daily confronted with people who have vowed not to forgive someone, somewhere because of words spoken. I have heard of people who would have preferred been physically assaulted, than verbally insulted! Words have powers to heal, or kill. No wonder most successful people today attribute their successes to the words spoken to them, or words they read at some points in their lives. This also applies to the failures we have today in the world. A lot of them would push the blame on ill words spoken to them, as they were growing up.

Some people are alive today because of the words spoken to them. Some have escaped suicide because they were encouraged, while on the other end of the divide are some, who committed suicide because of ill words spoken to them. Some, who were supposed to be successful, have decided against that, because of the kind of words their fellows used on them. A lot are into things they would naturally have avoided, because of wrong accusation. **"If they say I am this bad, then let me be bad, so that, I don't fill the guilt of the wrong accusations"**, they often encourage themselves.

A lot of businesses are dying today, because of the wrong usage of words and the power embedded in words. Customers are fleeing a lot of businesses all because they want to avoid coming in contact with certain words. Staffers are resigning also because of this evil. Successful business partners are parting ways, because of words wrongly used. It may interest you to know that " the tongues of fire" when first used in the Bible was on a positive note, it brought power of healing to those it fell on, and to those that they preached to, but then, they were under the guidance of a divine Being, who would not tolerate guile.

Those that received those cloven tongues of fire spoke so well that today there is nowhere in the world where their message is not taught and read. Fine, you may argue that these message dates over two thousand years ago, yet, we would all readily admit that their impacts are still been felt; healings are been received by merely reading and believing those words. Their tongues of fire spread like whirlwind and has established Christianity, as one of the major religions in the world today. Now, considered how your staff use their tongue – sorry – you inclusive! How have your business been helped, thus far? Are your tongues of fire, not repelling both partners and customers from your business?

You may wonder what tongue of fire has to do with your business, but the truth is that, daily, a lot of people are confronted with these tongues as they transact one business, or another. For a clarification, tongues of fire in the business world refers to: "Unethical usage of words to staff, colleagues, partners, clients in business dealings"

We have two major types of dealings, with respect to word usage. These are:

(a) Informal word usage
(b) Formal word usage

We use the former, when dealing with those we are either close to, or very familiar with. For the latter, undue familiarization is not allowed, word usage must, as much as possible, be official.

Our business world of today is more of the latter – communication is largely formal and official. It is a fast-paced world that has no room for triviality. You may note that, those that are involved in the business of jokes, or triviality – standup comedians do it in a very professional manner. Formal words are reduced to the minimal. They don't entertain by insulting their hearers. Those that engage in such practices are gradually losing their audience! Businesses are losing clients daily because of "tongues of fire" in the work place. Staff are depleting because of this evil. A lot of businesses are at the brink of collapse on this note. Why? Tongues of fire have eaten deep into the nerves of such businesses.

Words you rarely hear people use in offices in the past are freely being used today. Business owners have become demigods and are often so power-drunk that they feel they have to prove that they are the boss! There is guile in their words and members of staff are regularly insulted without due consideration to their feelings.

Recently I heard how a senior manager in an organization resigned all because the owner of the business uttered the following words:

"Without me you would not be what you are today".

This young man felt so insulted, and of course he was ready to not only lose the job, but if that meant him, losing everything and becoming poor, he was ready to embrace that path! So, he resigned.

Tongues of fire are killing businesses. As I write, resentment is building up on a daily basis against such businesses. One thing I realized lately is that some of the businesses that are folding up these days were as a result of the "tongues of fire". It might as well have been a case of two partners exchanging words, and in the process, what should have been kept secret was brought into the open. The resultant effect is a split. Now, you can imagine what would happen to such a business. Indeed, when the foundation is shattered, death is imminent. There is therefore, the need to consider some of those things that could be classified as tongues of fire, so that, you may know the direction your business is heading.

Characteristics of Tongues of Fire

Here, you want to know words that must be avoided, or carefully used.

You also would know some words that you must guide against and also prevent your staff from using. These words are so grievous that, to prevent their usage, you may need to penalize a member of staff who uses them. Failing to do this, will position your business for ultimate failure and eventual death. Please, note that, some positive words would also be introduced as the analysis continues.

(1) Tongues of Insult:

My belief is that, you have read this book to this extent because of the uplifting information you are getting. I am happy, that so far, you have not been offended. Insult comes when "someone speaks, or acts so as to offend another person".

Hey, you may need to pause here and consider how your business is run. You need to start this examination from yourself. Are the words you speak to your staff offensive or encouraging? Fine, you are the CEO, but you are not God. So you have your limits. Your ownership of the business does not give you the license to insult your employees. Mind you, when you insult your employees, they may not respond verbally, but one thing is certain – as much as is within their power, from that moment onward, they will be ready to partner with anything that will grieve you including the killing of your business.

So, if you are that CEO that is fond of insulting his staff, you are in a real trouble. This is, because, apart from the fact that they are grieved with you, you have, by your attitude; turn most of them into your business enemies! So you can imagine the outcome of a business that is being managed by its enemies – the

113

result would be sudden death. Something to make you marvel is that, if your business is thriving, it may be a function of your involvement, but the moment you are not there that business will collapse – no wonder we see a lot of businesses disappear as their owners die. The reason is not far-fetched. Such owners have assumed the position of God; failing to consider that one characteristic of God is that, He is immortal.

"A LOT OF BUSINESS OWNERS HAVE TAKEN THE POSITION OF GOD, FAILING TO REALIZE THAT UNLIKE GOD - WHO IS IMMORTAL - THEY WOULD ONE DAY DIE"

The advice therefore, is that, if you value your business so much, that you want it to thrive (with, or without you), then you must guard against this "tongue of insult". When you do that, you must also take out time to consider your employees. I am quite sure you would not spend a second longer on entering an office where the occupiers are insulting themselves.

Your business is toiling with failure, if it is characterized with people that see insult as a means of making their point. Recently I was watching a show, and I realized that one of the participants was resented by other participants and viewers, because he felt that the only way to make his point was through insult. O! How it turned out that he was loathed for that attribute.

Let's bring this back to your business; you already know that insult breeds resentment, conflict and enmity, so a business surrounded by these, is a house divided against itself. Such a house cannot stand. It would eventually crumble. Remember, the business is yours, and you are the most important person that can protect it. If this be the case, then a staff that feels that it is normal to insult others at will, (regardless of the position he, or she occupies) must be shown the way out.

How sad it is when I recall a statement made by one of my colleagues:

"Use your head."

Till date, I still remember that statement, but for my self-control and probably because of my person, I held myself back from responding. Fine, I did not respond immediately and I never retaliated, but anytime I remember that statement, I feel really bad. In fact, it makes me to steer clear of that person, as much as I can.

"Use your head" is an insult! You do not have the right, neither does your staff have that right to use that phrase for any reason. Using such expression means you probably failed to use yours before employing that person (I know you don't like that). That is exactly how people feel when you use such words on them (pardon me for I only wanted you to feel what such phrase could breed in others)! If my apology seems not accepted, you probably, at this point, feel insulted. And that is exactly what insults would do to your business! Again I tender my apology. I only use that to let you know that nobody likes to be insulted and it should be cleansed from a business.

The following are words and phrases to guide against. These phrases may stick to the minds of people for a long time and could create hate and resentment to your business. Ultimately, they would impact negatively on output and productivity:

1) Use your head.
2)   Think, think and think.
3)   I regret employing you.
4)   Without me, you are nothing.
5)   We are not on the same level.
6)   Who knows your family?
7)   I am the boss, yours is to follow.
8)   Who the hell are you?
9)   F-k you! (You must avoid the f – words).
10)   You are good for nothing.

11) **I doubt if you went to school.**
12) **Small boy (or girl).**
13) **You fool!**

The list of words to avoid is endless, but I will give you the key to note, and detect them. Any word that you would not like used on you, do not use it on others.

The Rule:

"DO UNTO OTHERS AS YOU WANT THEM TO DO UNTO YOU"

Insulting words must not and must never be allowed to thrive in your business in any of these forms:

1) Between you and your staff, partners and customers.
2) Between employee and employee.
3) Between staff and customer.
4) Between customer and customer.

Remember, the customer is like a visitor, you must not allow them to freely use guile words in your business arena, because onlookers may not know they are not your customers. So, you must realize that people are out there looking and don't want them to conclude in this manner:

"Don't go there if you don't want to be insulted."

(1) **Tongues of Curses:** This is slightly different from insults; it is a process where one violently utters abusive words, or call on evil to come on another person. The world is growing and civilization is fast spreading like wild fire; and unlike in times past, when people could openly lay a curse on another, such has reduced drastically. The sad truth is that, this drastic change has revolutionized the concept of cursing. What people do nowadays, is to

bewitch people in so much that, the recipient may be frightened and some may stoop to the extent of returning such curses to the sender.

The path to understanding this is to place it alongside the analysis given on insults. They are both related in some ways. Either way, their effects are harmful to the growth and sustenance of businesses.

One trait of an ailing and failing business is the prominence of curses. How do you want a business to progress, when words like the under listed are freely used?

1) My wish for you is that you die.
2) All my enemies, including you, will not prosper.
3) You will not live to see tomorrow.
4) Evil shall not leave your house.
5) You are bound to fail.
6) You will die in that position.

Any words used on another person, that wishes him failure, should not be allowed in your business. Where you or your staff is freely laying curses on each other, it simply means that, you are all at war with each other. Recall the saying: "When two elephant fights, it is the grass that suffers". In this case, the grass is your business.

Mind you, people cannot be forced to live their life in a particular way, but as far as your business is concerned, people could be regulated (through you or by you) to live to your standard or quit, if they choose not to obey the company policy.

(2) **Tongues of Quarrels:** The Bridge between insults and curses are quarrels. When people insult themselves; when people curse, this may lead to quarrels and the outcome, in most cases, is physical confrontation – fight. One sure

path to the death of a business is when that business gives room for people to insult, curse, quarrel, and fight. That is a lawless environment, and of course, no business would thrive in such an environment.

You need to lay down the example, by first not quarrelling with your staff. Instead, you can issue them a query. Your office is your business, and while you can quarrel in your homes (though, it could be avoided), the office is not a place for such. It is a formal environment and must be treated as such. There are rules for modulating behavior and resolving issues. Issuance of a memo or a query are some of the best options.

You do not want to turn your office into a place reputed for brawls. A staff must be taught the importance of a memo. They must be made to know, that the office is not a place where you quarrel, but there are acceptable and official ways of handling issues and as such, direct confrontation is never an option. So note these:

1. No quarrels between you, your staff and customers.
2. No quarrels between staff and customers.
3. No quarrels between customers in your business arena.

(3) **An Honourable Way:** Tongues of fire should not be allowed to truncate your business. The honourable ways to follow are:

1)   Be appreciative.
1)   Praise when needed.
2)   Pacify in and out of season.
3)   Hearsay should not be entertained.
4)   Busy bodies should have their place outside your business.
5)   Listening should be encouraged.

In concluding this segment, you need to note that:

"FOR HE THAT WILL LOVE LIFE AND SEE GOOD DAYS, LET HIM REFRAIN HIS TONGUE FROM EVIL, AND HIS LIPS THAT THEY SPEAK NO GUILE" (I PETER 3:10) KJV

Chapter Nine: The Killer Structures

In this segment, we shall consider physical and human structures, and how they act as business killers.

You have read a lot about behaviour that should be cut off from your business; you have read about word and their control; you have also read about specific groups of personnel that form your organization. All these have been tagged with merits and demerits. You must have also realized the role you play on the path of your business that might lead it to profit, or may cause that business to suffer loss and death. At first glance, one would think that these lessons are enough, for one to go back and overhaul his business. This intended overhauling of self and personnel will not cure the travail of an ailing business, when actually, the foundation of the business and its components are rested on some faulty structures, made up of human and physical structures.

If you are desirous, of not only creating a profitable venture, but a business that would stand the test of time, and eventually outlive you; then you must put a good structure in place that would sustain the business (with, or without you).

Mind you, a real business is one that runs itself (with, or without the owners' direct involvement). This not to say that, the owners are not relevant to the business; what I mean is that you can either, set up, or run a business that, moves when and only you are present, or you can set up a true business; one that is self-sustaining.

To attain this latter stage of business, which is the ultimate state business, it is essentially, a function of the structure in place. Let me take you on a trip to examine some of these structures that could keep your business afloat at all times and through all seasons.

In this regard, you shall get to understand some key structures, their impacts, as well as their merits and demerits. These shall be broken down into:

1. The Human Structures

2. The Physical Structures

The Human Structures: Every business, including those that may be completely mechanized or automated, has the human elements in place. Here the mechanized robotics or automated businesses are controlled by humans. When you set up a business as a sole proprietor, you, as a person, are involved. No matter the magnitude of a business, you cannot do without engaging the services of humans. And, in the case of a one-man business, the only person might be you.

If you would recall, a good business defined is one that, is profitable with growth. Growth, in this instance, implies more hands. More people would be engaged. When some businesses attain this level, instead of further growth, what happen is that, they begin to diminish. In other words, profit no longer equate to the output of the work force. But the truth is that, one should expect that, what one man does to attain certain height, more men should exceed that height. However, it is rather sad to note that a lot of businesses are going under, even with more employees. This is a function of lack of structure.

You may need to read *Small Business Big Life* by Luis Barajas, to learn how to organize your business and the team you need to set up. After doing that, it is needful that you sustain your business and prevent it from dying, by fully understanding the impacts that would be felt when a proper human structure is put in place; failure of which may be responsible for the plight of your business.

Now you think that you have a business – O! sorry, I should say: Now, you have a business: I rejoice with you. You have an office, I rejoice also with you. You have employees. Great! I continue to rejoice with you, but one thing I want you to realize is that, no matter the state of the growth, or profitability of your business, you don't have a business, if your business is devoid of a working structure. What you are doing could be termed as buying and selling. The moment you don't buy all the goods you want, you do not have anything to sell. Of course, this will affect your profit.

ANY BUSINEES WITHOUT A STRUCTURE, NO MATTER THE PROFIT IT GENERATES, IS A WALKING CORPSE –IT LACKS LIFE!

A business without a structure is a walking corpse – It lacks life. You may be tempted to think that your business is doing well. That means your structure is working, but mind you, a walking corpse has no life in it. It is dead and decomposing, and one day, the decay would overtake and overshadow the drift – so is your business.

You may need to consider these characteristic to save your business. A process that would help you to understand that your business may be dead and yet not decaying because it is under some preservatives; in this case, a flawed structure. This flawed structure would, if care is not taken, disgrace you at a time you least expect. Now consider them before they bring shame and loss to you.

Characteristics of the Killer Human Structure
1.   No Staff Training:

You may recall what you read about the Killer Receptionist – chapter six; the killer HR – chapter seven; and the killer customer care personnel, Marketers and sales representatives – chapter eight. You would recall reading about some killer behaviour, like wrong usage of words. The root causes of some of the ills, highlighted in the above-mentioned chapters, are functions of an organization that fails to train its staff. Quite a number of businesses are devoid of training. The impacts, are reflected, when you enter such business premises. What you see, are people, behaving in ways that suit them. Let me recount an experience.

I had a young undergraduate friend who requested to work with me, so I took him out on a business trip as a personal assistant. Mind you, this was a lad that was still in school. But I soon discovered that all he wanted was a holiday. We had known for some time, so my relationship with him was considered as a good basis to use him as my PA. Incidentally, this ended up as a bad idea.

I had taken this lad, because I felt it was cheap, but this almost cost my organization a contract, and so many benefits. The first traits was that, he still saw me as his friend – which I was, but failed to realized that the business world is not a convenient place to use nick-names, especially, when addressing your boss. In this case I was the boss. So as we progressed in our work, I called him by his nick-name and so also he did to me. And even though, that was not a problem, nonetheless, it naturally affected the business.

Secondly, this lad knew nothing about documentation and delivery of letter, and yet he was saddled with that responsibility. You can imagine the chaos this created. I recall once, when he was asked to issue a cheque that should be acknowledged, the ignorance he displayed was embarrassing. Regardless, this was not his fault. I will explain.

The big embarrassment came, when I was with a major client who noticed my relationship with my PA cum friend. He felt very embarrassed at our conversation. He called me aside and did express his reservations.

"You call that boy your PA?" He queried.

"Yes, he is," I had responded.

"If you know what is good for you and your organization, you better put him aside". He said angrily.

He later made me realize that, with the way my PA composed himself, both in our relationship and the nick-name he calls me, were way below the expectations of a serious business. Please note the words: "serious business." Thank God, I had someone who cared enough to draw my attention to that flaw that would have cost us so much. We did retrace our steps. Tutorials were given this lad, though insufficient, but it helped in averting a loss. You can see how lack of training can turn a serious business into "an unserious business", on the grounds of lack of proper or adequate training of their staff. In this regards, so many organizations that presently appear to be referred to as "unserious businesses"! Often, they employ staff and immediately saddle them with responsibilities the new employees know little or nothing about. Fine, the business may be thriving, but you can guess what would be going on in the minds of their customers and clients, each time, they are displeased with these companies' products and services, or their after-sales customer care.

Do you know that the show of ignorance by a company's staff and the display of unprofessionalism, are a function of lack of training? These may be creating a wrong impression of such a company's business, in the minds of its clients?

The implication is that, the company is dangling on the edge of the precipice, and may eventually collapse. Yet, this was not the wish of the promoters, or proprietors of the business, when it begun. However, to attain that initial goal, it would cost something, to save the business from crashing. If that reflects the current state of your business, then you need to train your employees before exposing them to the outside world.

You may have heard the words: "like father like son". So it is with business. Your employees' behaviour would be linked, not only to your business, but to your good self!

"LIKE EMPLOYER, LIKE EMPLOYEE!"

People tend to read your business from your behaviour, your products, your services and your staff's behaviour. So, an untrained staff, working for a trained CEO, would portray the CEO as untrained, because most of the businesses carried out by the CEO are done through the staff, and accordingly, people will equate their behaviour to that of the CEO. Therefore, as mooted earlier, training will cost you something, but would save you everything!

TRAINING YOUR STAFF WOULD COST YOU SOMETHING, BUT WOULD SAVE YOU EVERYTHING!

You don't just assume that your new employee is experienced and that he or she could resume at his or her duty post without the necessity of being trained. No! That would mean that you are running an unserious organization! Every organization must make it a priority to train their staff on a regular business. Here is a testimony:

You would recall that I narrated a story earlier on, in chapter six, about my encounter with a receptionist. Guess what, the last time I visited that office, I discovered that that lady had been promoted! The puzzle here was that, she had drastically changed! Her composure, manners and attitude to visitors had improved compared to what I earlier experienced! I probed and discovered that she had been sent for several trainings at home and abroad. The impacts of those trainings were evident in her behaviour. Till date, that change is fresh in my mind, and has completely replaced the earlier impression I had of her.

Pay something to save everything, including your good self! Remember the reason for setting up the business. You need to sustain the business at the level you have taken it. As more and more employees are coming in, you need to have them trained and retrained.

Train the office attendant, train the receptionist, train your secretaries, train the HR, train your managers, and train everybody. When you do, your business would be seen by all as a serious business. And like my encounter with the receptionist, you may be surprised that old customers or clients, who were planning to quit your business, are returning.

Do not allow your untrained staff to ruin your business. Apart from this, you also need to train yourself repeatedly. The reason for this is that what you think was right yesterday may be wrong today; a behaviour that was acceptable yesterday, may be rejected today; a template that was used yesterday, may have become outdated today; the words you used yesterday, that was gladly received , may be repulsive today. What is being insinuated here is that, trends are changing! Do not lock yourself and your business in a box. Training could be the saving grace that could bring you that big contract that has been eluding your organization. Do not be weary of training: train, train and train again, that is the key to a winning team.

2.   Lack of Staff/Duty Delegation:

You have seen how training impacts on your organization and others. One other thing that kills a business is the lack of appropriate staff and delegation. We see this, when a secretary begins to do the job of a cleaner, or a PRO begins to do the job of an HR. The success of a business is a reflection of its operations, in terms of duties and delegation. In my few years of working, since graduating from the university, I found myself working in organizations, where I was made to do everything and anything. You don't want to run your organization that way. This also, is a failure in terms of training. This is because, if your personnel are trained, duties would not be wrongly assigned. Everybody would know their nuts and would focus on cracking them.

A business devoid of delegation lacks merit. Duties must be tied to positions, and so it must remain. Everybody cannot do everything, things would go wrong, and what you will have at the end of the day is a staff handling a task incompetently. Ultimately, manpower would be wasted. But, if you delegate tasks and the right positions are filled with qualified staff, you would both save time and cost, and would ultimately increase profit and deliverables. This takes us to the next point.

3. Lack of Employees Manual:

Do you have one? I mean do you have employees manual? If you do, do you hand copy over to your employee upon employment? If you do, fine. But, do you update and review them regularly? Let's lace these questions with their possible answers and solutions. If you are presently running a business without issuance of employees' manual, that business will soon die. The reason why that, would happen, is because you don't yet have a business, in the real sense of the word. All you have done is to assemble people, to act and behave as they like, as situations present themselves. But, this can be greatly curtailed, if your employees have their copies of your company's employees` manual and are familiar with its content. This is to show you, how important employees` manual could be.

The employee's manual, is like your business constitution, which you refer defaulting staff to, whenever the need arises. Now, the question is: At what point, do you hand an employee a copy of the employee's manual? Do you hand copies of the employee's manual over to them at all? Please, note that, this ought to be done long before they commence work in your company. And if possible, run a test on the manual, to ascertain their knowledge.

Finally, how often do you update your employee's manual? Trends are changing very fast, and you can't afford to run your business on obsolete business practices. Your manual must be regularly upgraded, or updated to be in sync with the operational trend; to keep your business current and your staff properly fine-tuned. Your business hangs on how you run it, and it is therefore a function of your employee's manual. The advice here is that, if you don't have employees' manual, create one. If you do, hand it over to your staff. And finally, regularly update your employee's manual, so as to save your business from imminent collapse.

4.   **Undefined Hierarchy:**

Nature is governed by growth, and this takes place through various stages: You plant a seed; the cotyledons develop and growth follows through to maturity. The formation of man begins from the conception stages to the birth of the child; growth from infancy through the stages of adolescence to adulthood and then to old age. For both plants and humans – other organism inclusive – growth is a natural process, and when growth takes place it is usually not sudden. Rather, it is a process that progresses through stages. And depending on the present stages attained by individuals, we can then categorize them, according to their different stages of growth into different groups. For our present purposes, we can conveniently term these categories as hierarchies of seniority. But the most important aspect is that, they are differentiated by their functions, duties and obligations.

Hierarchy has to do with the different levels, as far as any activities are concerned. This process is very paramount in the business world. Atop the hierarchy of most businesses is the MD/CEO. When you go down the tree of a business organization, what naturally follows are the employees, or subordinates. Within the rank and file of employees, are different tasks and positional tags – that is, if the business in question is mindful of marked differentiations, as far as employees' positions are concerned.

You would recall the analysis on delegation, which purely centres on job specification. This was collaborated with our analysis on employees` manual, with respect to understanding one's task in an organization. For instance, an accountant should do the work of an accountant and also know the limits. The same also applies to other areas of operation.

Having the aforementioned, would elevate an office to a viable position. But a business that has all these, but lacks organizational hierarchy would not be fully optimized. On the other hand, an organizational hierarchy that is well designed is a plus for any business. Mind you, the keyword here is that such hierarchy must be well designed, but how? The answer is simple. A well designed organizational hierarchy is one that, ties positions with duties, responsibilities, salaries and other benefits. What this means, is that, the higher your position, the higher your salary and other benefits.

This definition needs no further explanation, just as natural hierarchies are naturally self-defining. For example, a full grow man and a new born baby. The difference between both, in terms of strength, understanding and perception is enormous. And therefore, as much is expected of a full grown adult, so also, must the reward tally with his experience. Let's bring this back to the business world. A lot of businesses are ailing today, because of the inadequacy of organizational hierarchy. Some organizations do not even have hierarchy in their operations, and when they do, the discrepancy in reward is so flawed that you wonder how such an organization would thrive in the long term. Some of the flaws you may detect in some organizations are:

1.   Lack of hierarchy.
2.   Undefined hierarchy.
3.   Inadequate rewards and benefits.

When you put these three together, this is what you get – an organization where you cannot differentiate employees by the positions they occupy because of the blurred line of reporting and the salary scheme. In a business, where the employees do not know the positions they occupy, they are not sure of their superiors because the overriding principle in that organization, is a scenario where a subordinate earns more than his superior.

The question therefore is that, how do staff work in harmony in such a flawed system? That apart, what also characterizes such an organization is the lack of drive and strives for promotion. This lag is a function of the lack of hierarchy, as the employees may not be so motivated due to the lack of operational hierarchy, so, there is nothing to work towards.

What you should realize at this point is that, when you run a business that does not motivate employees to aspire for promotion, your business merely exists, and may just be a place packed with activities carried out by men and women, with no option. And it would be obvious, that, if they have options, they will leave your organization, for one that is well structured. You may be deceived to think that, as long as you are making profit, that all is well. Sorry, to note that all is not well, because what would surprise you is that the profit you make could have been doubled, or tripled, if you have a well structured business.

Please, note that, the lack of proper hierarchy would negatively impact your business in the following ways:

1.   Your profit would become stagnant and after a period, you may be running at a loss. This is because stagnant profit would gradually get to a state of equilibrium, and with your expenses, which sooner, than later, would increase, would inevitably lead the business to a point, where it would begin to record losses, instead of profits.

2.   Your organization would be one filled with animosity. You can imagine this, yourself, when a subordinate earns more than his superior. The human tendency of pay back may set in, where people may not be mindful of their tasks, nor your business.

3.   One major setback, such an organization would experience, is the exit of staff. You know what it feels like, to lose a competent staff. The impacts are always dire.

Is your business ailing? Maybe you need to examine the lack of hierarchy or the flaws in the hierarchy you put in place. This you must do, in consideration of the various positions and your reward system. When you do this, the result would be tremendous. What you would get are happy employees – employees aspiring to grow, and a good working relationship between superiors and their subordinates.

What you may end up with is a system where your employees fully give of themselves to your business and excellence, knowing full well, that, such would be adequately rewarded financially, or through promotion.

Finally, on the killer human structure, you need to guide against the aforementioned odds, if your business is thriving. But if otherwise, adhere to the advice given, and your ailing business would be revived.

(B) The Physical Structures
You have seen five hazards of a flawed human structure. Here, you need to know the hazards of a flawed physical structure.

The difference between the human structure and physical structure is that, the human structure is more internal in your business, and may also be private to you and your staff; but the physical structure are apparent to the outside world. When you talk of physical structures, you are referring to the space, gadgets and tools used in running your business.

PHYSICAL STRUCTURES REFERS TO THE BUSINESS ENVIRONMENT

How are the physical things used in running your business maintained? What you may note is that, People that do business with you by contact may first be confronted with your business environment. This also creates the first and lasting impression.

Let's do this little exercise: Suppose you enter a restaurant for the first time, and the first thing you are confronted with is a foul odour. And though, this is enough for a lot of people to turn back, yet you decided to patronize them. Suppose it turned out that, the first seat you tried to sit collapsed; you got an apology from the waiter, who directs you to another table that had been used, with the dishes, serviettes, water, yet to be cleared and the surface of the table cleaned, necessitating you to beckon to a waiter, to clear the table. Suppose, the waiter you beckoned, came with apology and clears the table, after which you place your order, but then, you discovered that the waiter is ill-dressed. And as if these were not enough, it turned out that, when your order is eventually served, it is served in cracked plates, and the glass supplied for you to drink, is slightly broken at the rim, what would be your reaction?

At this point, a lot of people would be extremely displeased to the point that they would leave the restaurant, in a huff. But for the purpose of this exercise, suppose you managed to eat the meal, made payments and left, would you ever return to that restaurant again? Or would you refer someone to that restaurant? I know your answer is obviously NO. The next question is: Do you think such a restaurant would survive? This also, is an obvious NO. Such a business is at the brink of collapse, its death is imminent, and this is how a lot of businesses die.

Most business owners start well, but the problem is with continuity. They start with renting a good office space. They renovate the office, paint it, buy new furniture; electrical appliances are changed, new cooling systems are fitted; chairs, tables and even the landscape are properly put in place, after which the business kicks-off. Two years and counting, these things they have put in place begin to decay and nothing is done about them. Fine, they may have practical knowledge of the business; their clients and customers have increased, and yet they may appear not to be bothered about the decaying physical structures.

So what happens next? Such a business; if care is not taken would get to a state where their customers' growth starts diminishing, and profitability may be affected. The reason for this is not far-fetched. It may be easier for an existing customer not to be mindful about your decaying structure, since he already does business with your organization, but do you think a new client, or customer would understand that? Of course, no serious minded customer would enter a disorganized office, or would want to do business with such an organization. The point here is that, your shabby environment could turn-off a prospective client!

Some time ago I overheard someone saying that: "If you go to that office, you had better not use their toilet".

You can imagine if this is the kind of statement an intended client hears about your organization. What do you think his reaction would be?

One salient point to note is that, no matter your product, the environment that houses that product matters a lot. You need to take the maintenance of your business environment seriously, just as much as you care for your business.

Things about Your Physical Structures that Can Kill Your Business

1.　　　　　　**The Killer Landscape**

It is a well known fact that there is healing in a good landscape. This is the reason it is advised that flowers be planted around medical facilities. You don't want to lose your customer because of an ill-kept environment. You may not know the number of prospective customers your business environment (landscape) has caused to turn their backs on your business. Poorly trimmed flowers, ill-kept drainage and depleting water ways could negatively impact on either an existing customer, or a prospective one. You can afford to lose what you don't yet have, but you can't afford to lose your existing customers.

Here is how your ill kept surrounding impacts negatively on your existing customers: it may create an impression that your business is failing, and once such an impression is created, be rest assured that such a client may start planning to find and patronize a competitor, that offers the same product or service as you, plus a serene environment. I guess you wouldn't want that to happen. So, if you don't want to lose both your prospective and existing clients and customers, you must be environmentally conscious.

2.　**Depleting Paints**

When last did you paint your office wall? Do you know that a failing paint conveys a wrong signal about your business? Just like the latter, it creates the impression that your business is failing, and you may also be losing some of your customers as a result of this.

3.　**The Killer Reception**

You may recall what was said about the killer receptionist in chapter six. Your reception is as important as your receptionist, and the whole of your business.

How would you feel if you enter the reception of an office only to find out that the whole place is in disarray? For instance, the floor is ill-kept; rugs or carpets are decaying, the chairs are broken, and the receptionist desk is not appealing. Would you be inspired to do business with such an organization? I guess, you would largely be discouraged and you may not have the guts to continue. Obviously, doubts would have set in, about the seriousness of the business owner!

Your reception paints very strong impressions about your business. I guess you don't want to paint a picture before them that tells that your business is distressed, even if your business is distressed. Remember that a distressed business was one time stress free. Therefore, it needs clients and customers to take it back to that level. So, you don't want your distressed reception area to scare a prospective visitor away from patronizing your products, or services.

4.   The Killer Lavatory

An unclean lavatory could portray your business in a wrong light. Here, the focus is not solely on the lavatory, you need to see it from the perspective for which this book is intended – impression creation.

Reference is being made, here, to your lavatory because your business must be protected, and you do not want an unclean lavatory to create a wrong impression about your well crafted business. You must guide your business against all odds, including impressions that are wrong about your business.

Humans generally are sensitive to faults. There is trouble when a fault is not guarded against, no matter how insignificant that fault may be. It may create an effect of great devastation. The point to note here is that, most of the collapsed structures we have experienced the world over are traceable to small faults – a bolt that is not well screwed; a nail that was not properly hammered into place; leakage that was not sealed up on time…. All these are small faults with grave consequences. The wisest man that ever trod this earth said: in one of his write ups, that:

"Wisdom is better than weapons of war: BUT ONE SINNER DESTROYETH MUCH GOOD". (Ecclesiastes 9:18).

Just like a information can change the life of a man, so also one mistake can destroy everything that man has spent his life building. Your lavatory has such power of destruction! Keep it clean. Keep it safe. Your business depends on it.

5. The Killer Appliances:

Your electrical appliances play a major role in portraying your business as safe. You may need to change that blinking fluorescent tube, noisy AC, faulty fan and dead television set. Why keep an appliance that is faulty? That shows lack of organization and maintenance. You want your client and your customer to discuss business with you, yet your cooling system is not functioning well. A meeting is shortened because the environment is not conducive, or comfortable.

Your partners, clients and associates have assembled for a crucial meeting and all they are confronted with, is an unappealing conference room, all because, you have failed to put your cooling system in order. Here is what would happen: most attendees would rather make their point hastily, so that, they could leave that environment. And do you know the consequence of that? Decisions would also be made hastily, which would negatively impact on your business.

Know and note these:

  i.   If an appliance is bad, it should not be kept.
 ii.   A blinking fluorescent tube should be changed as soon
         as possible.
iii.   The adequacy of your cooling system is a necessity.

Finally, cleanliness should be your watchword. A neat office with fewer gadgets is preferred to a fully automated office that is untidy.

YOUR BUSINESS DEPENDS ON YOUR STRUCTURES. KEEP IT FUNCTIONAL. KEEP IT CLEAN. MAINTENANCE IS MANAGEMENT.

You don't want a serious business to be depicted as one that is unserious, because it is operating under a decrepit structure.

Chapter Ten: The Killer Customer(s)

I still remember how my mother started her bread business with so much zeal and commitment. As an educationist, she wanted more from life and her credentials, though great, was not meeting her heart desire, so she veered into business.

Her choice of business was purely hers and she plunged headlong into the business – a business I saw grew from scratch into a thriving one. Her stocks increased; her customers increased; her income increased; and my allowances increased too. She put in all her life, and part of mine, into that very business. Then suddenly, I saw her accounts book grow from one to several. Were they accounts of her customers, deliveries, profits or debts? I often thought. They were the lists of her customers. They had grown tremendously, but unfortunately the business had taken most of her time, and was threatening to take her joy too. As numerous as her customers were, most were indebted to her.

What I realized at that stage, her business had gotten at the time was that, while she had succeeded in increasing her customer base and sales, most of her funds were outside. Fine, her customers had increased, but most of them were bad customers – people who took goods on credit and refused to pay. So, she was saddled with debtors. Before my very eyes, I saw life being sniffed out of her business. Day and night, I saw my mother struggling to collect her money from her debtors, most of whom, were either unwilling to pay, or could not afford to pay. Gradually, I saw her stock deplete and eventually disappeared. Eventually, my mother was left with one thing – the list of debtors! Her money was outside. As I write, that business died over ten years ago. Yet, my mother still has, in her custody, that list. When we drive around town, she would always draw my attention to some of her debtors or their residences. Ironically, most of them had died!

I cannot forget that period of our life and the fact that our main source of livelihood was killed by the most important constituent of the business – our customers! Indeed, customers are the backbone of any business. But if your business is saddled with the wrong customers, the end of that business is near.

Now, you may blame the owner of the business for running the business on credit, but you must also realize that in the business you can't afford not to deal with those who want some form of credit. And indeed, you must have been indebted to others at one time, or the other. It would appear then that the main reason why we have banks is that, you can always approach them and apply for credit facility when you have a project, or contract to execute and do not have the funds required to execute it. So it is, with a lot of businesses. Somehow, they are compelled to offer some credit to their devoted customers and clients, in the form of 'buy now and pay later' arrangements. Interestingly, I have been to places with stickers on the wall that read:

"NO CREDIT TODAY, COME TOMORROW".

What a great slogan that is! But how many businesses operate without dealing with debtors? One thing, I want you to realize is that, the greatest corporations in the world today are somehow indebted. In addition, they have debtors as well. The case may be that, they are credit worthy, or that their debtors are credit worthy. But the fact still remains that, taking of loan, or goods and services on credit is a major part of the business world.

Now, who are your customers?

Your business is at the verge of collapse and might soon die, that is, if most of the customers you have are indebted to you, or if most of the services you render were rendered, in the belief that you would be paid later.

Let's get this fact very clear, lots and lots of businesses from time immemorial have been killed by this business killer – customers. A lot of banks have folded up in recent times, because of bad customers – those they granted loans (with, or without collaterals), who failed, or could not afford to pay back the loans they obtained from the banks.

The present economic meltdown the world is presently going through, accompanied with cases of mental, physical illness and suicides are a function of indebtedness. Before the meltdown, the business world was thriving. Lots of people channeled all their savings and earnings into investments. Loans were taken and banks granted loans to individuals, cooperate organization and investors to invest in the stock market, with little, or no collaterals, save their equity holdings in the stock market.

Then, suddenly, there was a whirlwind. Economic saboteurs invaded the world. Stock markets suddenly began a downward spiral. It was so bad that, investors wanted to sell their stocks but found out that, there were no buyers. Prices of stocks plummeted. The business world came under attack, and all we could do was watch as events unfolded. It became apparent that the foundation on which most the businesses were built was speculative, run by haters of due process and order. These became their killers.

Finally the world came to a standstill; banks found themselves indebted. Equally, the real estate sector was not left behind; mortgages were failing because most credit facilities could not be serviced by customers indebted to them. Business killers had caught up with a lot of them – the killer customers!

In shame, some affected persons decided to commit suicide. Some just disappeared. A lot of banks are in court, contending the viability of collateral that cannot secure 10% of the loan granted. Evidently, banks had lost good sums of money. Borrowers had debtors and stock traders that could not secure the loans they obtained from the banks. Then suddenly, great corporations were folding up. Consequently, governments all over the world began working round the clock, to generate bail-out funds. Billions of dollars were pumped into the economy, to salvage it from total collapse.

The world is at war, but this time it is the occupants that are at war with themselves. Businesses were entered into with good intentions, but those intentions have been thwarted by situations that were created by none other, than the decisions of business owners, and their customers and clients that have become the greatest threat to their businesses. Goods taken, are not being paid for; loans taken, are not been serviced; and services rendered, are not also paid for. Customers have now become business killers, by default.

The aforementioned issue is one that has touched all residents of the planet earth, but life must go on. Whilst old businesses are folding up, new businesses are emerging to take their place. This is because life itself is a measure of business. The crucial questions at this point are: How is your business? How are your customers? Hope your business is not one that rested on debtors? Hope your transactions are not on debts?

You are running a business that could end up being killed by the customers, if all you have, are customers that patronize your business on credit. It is better, you don't have a customer at all, than having customers that are debtors – they will kill your business. Another category of the killer customers are displeased customers.

Throughout this book, clarification has been made, that the customer must be pleased at all cost on the grounds that, the major reason for setting up your business – aside profitability – is to satisfy any customer that, patronizes that business.   Now imagine a business that fails to satisfy its customers. What do you think would happen to that business? It will die.

A BUSINESS THAT FAILS TO SATISFY ITS CUSTOMERS WILL DIE

If anything goes awry with your business it must not affect your customers' satisfaction. The reason for this, as earlier stated, is that one aggrieved customer equates thousands of aggrieved customers and prospective customers. The world is changing and quite a lot of businesses are changing with it; some positively, while a lot are changing negatively. **Let's focus on the negative change that has impacted negatively on some businesses, relative to their customers.**

It is sad to note that more and more businesses seem not to be taking cognizance of the fact that customer satisfaction is *key*. Consider the experience my sister in law had recently. She had bought a brand new phone from a shop, but less than a week it developed a fault. On returning the phone – instead of the phone being replaced at no extra cost, she was made to pay some money, for the phone to be repaired. And since she had no choice, she had to give in.

It would appear that one thing those people failed to realize is that though they had proven to be smart, yet they have lost, not just one customer, but many other potential customers, she probably would have told others about their services by word of mouth, or that would have seen the phone with her and would have wanted to know where she had made the purchase. Do you think she would refer them to that shop? No way.

Secondly, that shop has created problems not only for itself but the manufacturers of that phone. So you can imagine the chain of reaction a service poorly rendered can have on a business and the products it markets. So then, a single displeased customer is more than enough to kill a business!

A SINGLE DISPLEASED CUSTOMER IS MORE THAN ENOUGH TO KILL A BUSINESS!

You would have probably heard people vow not to enter a particular shop or office again. Some even vow not to patronize certain products. You need to find out from the few customers that still patronize you, how best they think you can best serve them.

Let me conclude with a short story of an occurrence that took place in the real estate sector. Agent A and B (for purpose of confidentiality I shall refrain from mentioning names), entered a business deal. The property was eventually disposed off and agent A refused to pay agent B, as agreed. Agent B, being a gentleman, took the matter kindly. But it happened that sometime later, nemesis caught up with agent A. Agent A soon had a wealthy client. He had, in fact, sealed a deal with the client that was worth a fortune. Unfortunately for agent A, fate brought his client in contact with agent B. Agent B was discussing with another colleague, on how he was cheated by agent A and why he would never do business with him. He had complained bitterly about how untrustworthy agent A was.

Unknown to agent B, the man standing beside him was a client to agent A, his former business partner. It transpired that when agent A's client heard this, he made enquiries and found out, that the agent who was being talked about was the agent he had sealed a deal with, and was at the verge of making payments to. Immediately, agent A's client called off the deal. He then handed the brief to agent B, who, at the time, was unknowing sharing a sad experience in the hearing of agent A's client. I don't know if agent A got to know what transpired. What is certain, is the fact that agent A was responsible for his misfortune. He displeased just one client and lost the big kill.

Your clients, customers, partners and whosoever patronizes your business are crucial to the success of that business and they must, at all cost and at all times, be pleased. This is because, you don't know how many of your customers and prospective customers would be lost when you displease one.

A fact to note is that, one displeased customer, client, partner, or associate would not only kill your business, but in a sense, kill you! A lot of people have lost their lives because they had cheated someone, or displeased the customer.

A DISPLEASED CUSTOMER WOULD NOT ONLY KILL YOUR BUSINESS BUT IN A SENSE, KILL YOU!

The greatest advice for all time focuses on "one" thing:

"A WORD IS ENOUGH FOR THE WISE"

Notice that in some cases, one customer is enough for your business, so please your customer(s).

Chapter Eleven: The Killer Manager/Leader

The manager that knows not, and fails to realize that he doesn't know, and yet is puffed up and would not give in to reason, nor sound judgment, is like an ignited grenade that leaves nothing within close range safe. Your business would run into trouble, when it is rested in the hands of the aforementioned – a killer manager.

Get this very clear, you have a killer manager running your business. It is like trying to make an assassin that had been assigned to kill you your bodyguard. Suffice to say that the greatest teacher and leader of all-time described a leader as a servant. Hear Him:

"He that is greatest among you shall be your servant".
(Matthew 23:11).

This statement was exemplified throughout the short period He spent on this earth. He refused to be called master. He refused the title of a teacher. He refused anything that would elevate Him. Rather, He lived His life serving people, until He died a shameful death. You may begin to wonder where all these are taking us to. Is your business ailing? Your management team and leaders might be leading your business to its death, if they see themselves as the leaders and the bosses rather than as servants. So what? Is a manager not supposed to walk as the boss? Should he stoop to the level of a messenger? You ask. Good questions.

True, a manager and a leader should walk like the title connotes. And indeed, Richard Templar writes, that we should "walk the walk" – that is, that we should walk the way a manager walks. But you should also note that walking the walk does not mean you should elevate yourself to the level of a demigod or "The untouchable" as typified in movie so titled, starring Kelvin Costner, in a tale that saw the untouchable gang lord being touched.

The managers and leaders of your business should portray themselves, as their job prescribes, but it must not be done in pride. Pride will yield a negative result on the grounds that such a leader would hardly give ears to reason. In addition, he probably won't humble himself to learn, even when he does not know, and as such, he would think himself all-knowing. He may constantly take wrong decisions and issue wrong instructions to his subordinates. He may end up, defending a failed system because his pride would not let him succumb to reason.

Recall, that your business is your business, and it was set up because you wanted it to sustain, not only you, but others. Should this be the case, you need to be careful of the kind of leaders you put in charge of your business. Lots and lots of businesses are ailing while some have crashed because, such businesses were left in the hands of killer leaders – people that had more interest in the position they occupied than in the business they were employed and assigned to manage. You need to know the traits of killer managers, or leaders, so as to save your ailing business, or prevent your business from death.

Characteristics of the Killer Managers/Leaders
(1). Proud and Arrogant:

Sometimes, issues become complicated, not necessarily because they could not be addressed, but because ego gets in the way. The following are typical of most failed businesses: "I am the boss, whether you like it or not, what I say is final!" the MD says, rather imperially.

The above statement comes from an all-knowing boss, until the creditors came and took over the business. Yet, he maintains his position. "I have done no wrong, I did my best. I made sure the staff obeyed my instruction." He insists, nonetheless.

"Where has all these landed us now?" the CEO queries.

The bossy boss is mute. Then, it strikes the MD that the business he thought he was running was already dead and buried, courtesy of his pride and arrogance.

One thing I know, is that pride and arrogance, especially on the part of the overseer of a business would ultimately lead to the untimely death of that business. Don't say I said so. I am not the originator of that statement. It is just a subtle way of quoting the all-time best instructor – Solomon:

"PRIDE GOETH BEFORE DESTRUCTION AND A HAUGHTY SPIRIT BEFORE A FALL." (Proverbs 16:18).

Let's come to how this negatively impacts on your business. You may also be guilty of these traits! So align yourself with the analysis. First, answer these questions:

i.   Do you or your managers believe that you know more about your business than the employees?

ii.   Are you and your managers' instructions "yea and amen"?

iii.   Does your managers' presence evoke fear rather than, respect in your employees?

iv.   Are you, or your managers too busy to listen to complaints from members of staff?

v.   Are there paths, lifts, or other facilities in your business premises that are restricted to you, or managers use only?

Let's pause here. You can generate more of such questions. Interestingly, these questions are being asked, to help you detect, if you or your managers are running your business with pride and arrogance.

What is your answer to the first question? If you think you know more about anything relative to others, it is not a bad feeling, but if this feeling is not managed properly, the outcome could be disastrous, especially in relation to a working environment.

Even if you know and think you know much more than others, because of the actions you may have taken in the past that yielded negative results, which you now term mistakes – you should listen to the suggestions and opinions of others. "I know better than thou" manager or an"all knowing manager" may be ignorant. And because he or she feels that way, uninformed instructions may be imposed on others. Here is an example of the "all knowing" manager: A meeting is called and he is the only one that does all the observations and talking. To him, a meeting was called but in actual fact, he had only assembled his staff to pass on instructions – wrong or right. Then, when things begin to go wrong, he finds out (if he is honest with himself), that he wanted to force a right outcome from a wrong input!

A manager that carries himself as all-knowing will most likely kill your business. The truth is that, there is no all-knowing individual on this earth. That is, the reason we have so many professors in a particular field – what one professor may know, another professor may be ignorant of, and yet, both of them are professors in their same field! That you are to manage people in a line of business does not make you the custodian of all information, statistics and data about the business. You must realize that the duty of a manager is to guide, assist, and advice, on the smooth running of the business. Alas! If you think you know all about the business, you would fail in those duties. And when you impose the wrong instruction, a wrong outcome will manifest.

If you, or your manager is proud and arrogant, and if your instructions are "yea and amen," there would be no room for clarification. The MD, having spoken, expects that his instructions would be carried out to the letter, regardless of whether those instructions are wrong. But the fact is that, if the eventual outcome would negatively impact on the business and everyone would suffer the effects. Wouldn't it have been better and proper to table the matter before all, rather than, incurring avoidable hazards, for all to suffer? Fine, you are meant to be followed, but you need not create an environment that would make it difficult for your staff to draw your attention to the consequences of some of the instructions you have given.

A "yea and amen" type of instruction is only applicable to God, but if you and your team of managers decide to assume that role, then you must realized that unlike God who can change times and seasons, and even upturn things without a thought, you lack such capabilities. Does your presence or the presence of your managers create fear rather than, command respect from your associates and subordinates? Imagine a scenario where the MD is coming and members of staff stiffen up. Some who had wanted to recline a bit from the stress of work and mental engagement suddenly had to start working, for the fear that they might be reprimanded for being idle. The truth of the matter is that, you are running a business that would soon crash!

A business environment should be a place where people do their job, and if sentiments must be applied, then, it must be that of respect, and not fear. It is surprising to see a manager pride that members of staff and subordinates are afraid of him. The consequence of this is that, what would be done when the MD is present might be left undone, in his absence! As earlier noted, fear creates hate and resentment, and a business would eventually crumble if its environment is laced with resentment and hate.

The proud and arrogant manager wants to be feared, and in so doing would make a lot of rash decisions. He may even end up sacking the wrong staff, to prove how powerful he is, forgetting that his strength rests on the success of the business, which his pride and arrogance is killing, by installment.

Indeed, you have killer managers in your business, if they are too bossy to listen to complaints or advice from their subordinates. They may even transfer same to clients and customers. Recently a friend shared his experience with me. He had spoken with the manager of a hotel on a business deal. The manager had requested for a proposal. He did that and included a covering letter addressed to the manger of the hotel. It turned out that the manager sent back the letter and refused to see my friend. The display of impunity infuriated my friend, so much, so that, as he narrated his ordeal, I felt his pain with equal intensity that, I became persuaded that, if that hotel were the only hotel in the whole universe, I certainly would not patronize them!

Is your manager so characterized – one that has become so big that his ears are shut to all and sundry? In fact, one that cannot listen to others has disqualified himself from the managerial seat. Unfortunately, lots of managers have this larger than life image. They feel that, subordinates must be kept far from them. To them, distance makes all the difference. Fine, they may keep the distance, but let them communicate through phone calls. And it is important, to point out that, since they are managers, then they must listen to their subordinates!

The proud and arrogant manager creates segregation in the business arena. Certain forms of restrictions are good in a business, but an unnecessary chasm need not exist between managers and members of staff. Pride and arrogance would create unnecessary friction, a gaping gulf, and ultimately an ailing business. Times are changing real fast and your business must change with it. Gone are the days of slavery, when slaves must steer clear of their masters' paths. Today, civilization has overtaken all that. But if your business is still running on such archaic conditions, then soon and very soon, the negative outcome would tell on your business.

(2) Simple and Ignorant:

This trait is a contrast to the latter. Recently I have been researching on God's view, on pride and arrogance. I hope to one day, make a detailed compilation of my findings. But let me summarize my discovery:

THERE IS NO ESCAPE ROUTE FOR THE PROUD AND ARROGANT PERSON

I discovered that, God hates pride and arrogance. I turned to simplicity and ignorance and guess what I discovered – God detests them. I also did find out that the proud and arrogant man places himself higher than where he belongs, while the simple and ignorant man does not recognize the importance of his position and so, is not conscious of certain developments that may significantly affect him one way, or the other. He is not moved at all – whether bad or good – he swallows all to his destruction.

Now consider your manager: Is he proud and arrogant, or simple and ignorant? Note that a manager that fails to distinguish himself from his subordinates falls into the latter category and may jeopardize your business. A key element of such a person is that, he is ignorant of the office he occupies. Unlike the former that forces his thought and ideas on others without reasoning with them, the simple and ignorant manager has no clear-cut idea of what he wants to achieve, and so he is largely controlled, or manipulated by his subordinates. Unlike the former, where the subordinates live under constant fear, the space overseen by the simple and ignorant manager is a lawless place. Members of staff behave as they please. The reason is not far-fetched – their manager is ignorant of how the business environment should be.

A great number of organizations fall into this category, where incompetent and unskilled personnel are saddled with managerial positions. The result is gross display of ignorance. This state of affairs, when displayed outside to clients and customers, could negatively affect the business and lead to significant losses.

Man is prone to misunderstand simplicity and ignorance, and may think that the simple and ignorant person is humble. This assumption is wrong. Humility makes one tolerant and understanding. A humble person listens to conflicting views, and would take practical steps to enforce right, while striving to persuade everyone to follow suit without getting on their nerves. On the other hand, the simple and ignorant person does not know how to engage people, even though he may appear to listen to others sometimes, yet, the choice of actions would be left to others.

An office managed by the simple and ignorant manager, as earlier stated, is a lawless set up. You may be surprised, to see the manager doing the job of an office assistant, even though the office assistant is there idling away. To him, it does not matter. But, what you would have at the end of the day are two groups of staff – the overworked staff and the idlers. It wouldn't be long, when strife and internal wrangling would become noticeable. Is your business so characterized, you need to examine the man managing it. He may lack the necessary skills and core competencies of a manager. You could – in a way – be able to determine whether your management team is in disarray.

Unlike the proud and arrogant manager, that is quick to assert that his idea and instruction helped the company earn a fortune, the simple and ignorant manager naturally passes the bulk of responsibilities to his subordinates. If the owner of the business falls into the latter category, then, it is a tragedy. In most cases, because of inadvertence, or ignorance, a staff may be wrongly accused.

A business owner must realize that, the first person that must take the blame if anything goes wrong in a business is the leader. This is one of the key tenets of leadership. Unless the leader did all he could, to avoid the damage that resulted, but his subordinates – against clear instructions – acted in a manner that occasioned the loss suffered by the business, then crucifying a staff, while leaving the manager is certainly not the right step. But a lot of businesses are so characterized. The reason is not farfetched. The business owner wants to save face. Consequently, he knows that when the manager he appointed is accused, the same finger would eventually point to him, so the scapegoat is a junior staff. The consequence of this development is that, a feeling of resentment and distrust is created amongst members of staff. Eventually, what becomes paramount in their hearts is to do, as they like, because whether they are to blame, or not, the blame would eventually fall on them. If your business is so characterized, it is treading the path of death.

What you should do from henceforth, is to examine the competence of your manager, if you discover that things are going wrong in your business. A simple and ignorant manager will always present to you, a staff that has defaulted, or created a problem. If this is the case, why don't you ask him where he was when such action complained about, was going on? At this point, you may be surprised to discover how ignorant your manager is.

The simple and ignorant manager is a killer that must be stopped from wrecking havoc in your business. But to stop such a killer in his tracks, you need to be extremely careful. This is because; such a manager may be loved by the staff of your business. Now tell me, who won't love a manager that allows him, or her do whatsoever he pleases? A child would naturally, gravitate to and become fond of a parent that allows him to do as he likes. And of course you already know where such indulgence could lead a child. Such a child would become spoilt by default, and would predictably go on to bring pains and shame to his or her family. Is your manager overtly loved by his subordinates? Mind you, it is a very good thing to be loved by one's subordinates. But in your case, does this display of love and affection enhance productivity, or occasion losses to your business? If the latter is the case, you have a killer manager handling your business affairs. Consequently, this would be like that of the spoilt child that brings pains and shame. Your business is at risk!

The keys have been handed to you, to shut out this killer from your business, or live with the consequences.

(3) The Ostentatious Manager:

I still remember the advice I was given when I recounted that, my little daughter would eat all through the night, and then, continue in the day. I was told that it was good for the child to eat, eat and eat again; that, this would help her health and growth. Whereas, it is good for a child to eat repeatedly, however, for your manager, this would be a killer trait that is guaranteed to plunge your business into unprecedented losses.

The ostentatious manager is a pleasure seeker. And what does the pleasure seeker do often? Of course, he would do anything that would bring him pleasure! This is always his target. Consequently, such a manager would be up, dragging you into unnecessary financial deals, guaranteed to bring him gain, rather than, increase the fortunes of your business. He always feels his unsearchable appetite must be gratified.

He loves life on the fast track; friends with insatiable taste for flashy things. He loves to live large and spend big. He loves expensive clothing, and flashy cars. As a matter of fact, everything about him must speak of grandeur. He is always chasing the big kill, but would never succeed at making that kill. All he is interested in is that funds be released to him for travelling and other sundry expenses. Is your manager ostentatious? You have a killer manager in your business! Mind you, the strength, or success of your business is not measured by the look of your manager, but by the feat they accomplish – helping your business attain milestones of sustained profits and growth.

You have a killer manager in your business, when all he is interested in, is the creation of a false impression about your business. Your business is ailing and instead of your management to proffer solutions to the problems, someone is telling you to protect the image of an ailing business. Tell me, how can you protect the image of a business by making a false press release? Again, let's say fraud has been detected in your business and you find your manager telling you that such information must not be let out, but that you should conceal the problem, instead. You may do that, but mind you, what you have succeeded in doing is covering your injury with a plaster; the injury has not healed.

Is your business filled with employees that would rather spend their time protecting the image of the business, rather than thinking of ways of helping the business make profit? Is your management staff ostentatious? What they are after is to project their personal image at the expense of your business. Eventually, it is your business that suffers. What are you afraid of, in reaching a decision on who to keep and who to send packing? What image are you protecting? Or is the business no longer yours? Or sad still, are you ostentatious?

Indeed, a lot of businesses that have gone under had ostentatious owners – those that would rather portray a big picture of an ailing business to the public, forgetting that they are actually concealing decay. But the truth is that, you may conceal decay, but you cannot conceal the odour.

YOU MAY CONCEAL DECAY BUT YOU CANNOT CONCEAL ODOUR

Ostentatious lifestyle of business owners and their managers has killed a lot of businesses. And indeed, quite a lot of present-day businesses run by persons who are materialistic are actually dead. More branches may be opened, fleet of luxury cars may be purchased, expatriates may be engaged, but these steps alone are not sufficient in themselves, to keep afloat a business that is going under. Eventually, such businesses are declared insolvent.

One fact that must be noted is that, if there is one life that is very expensive to sustain, it is ostentatious lifestyle. It is very expensive because of the price that goes with it. It is a life that is prone to fraud, theft, lies, falsehood, deceit, etc. You must realize that the business is yours and that, if it goes down, it will drag you along. So, do not allow another person create that ugly situation for you. Take pragmatic steps to save your business from these killers.

(4) Sexual Predators:

Immorality in any guise must not be allowed in your organization, especially amongst your management team. This is because lots and lots of businesses are failing because sex has been allowed to control how such businesses are run. There is no subtle way to put this, because your primary mission is to protect your business from being killed. If there is one killer trait in a manager, then that trait is guaranteed to ruin your business, unless you deal with it. And one of the gravest of such threats is what I would like to refer to as insatiable sexual appetite.

Let's start from the very beginning – recruitment. Who are those being recruited by your management team? Are they those that have traded themselves for the job? Is your manager someone, who will easily give away your business in exchange for sexual gratification? If you are not sure, then you need to examine the competence of their staff in-take.

There is a grave danger, if employees are absorbed, not on the basis of merit, but because they've offered 'something' for the job. The consequence is that, you would end up with staff that, behaves unbecoming, repeatedly. Such an employee might boast in the following words, "If the MD is with me, what can anybody do to me?" By reason of this anomaly, superiors are not respected and job done by junior workers, at their pace and in a manner they choose – at the expense of the business.

Is your business ailing? If it is, then you need to critically examine your staff intake. Are they employed because they have the required qualifications, or the technical know-how? Or they are employed because sexual appetite has beclouded the boss' sense of judgment? You are a business owner, so I don't need to probe further as regards these issues. One thing, I would like to make clear at this point is that, scores of marriages, families, friendships and associations have come under serious attack by this singular evil. This insatiable sex appetite has led to break-ups and divorce. Sadly, this evil has also crept into lots of businesses and has killed quite a number of them. Some are under their severe grip, and if there is one grip that is hard to break loose from, it is the grip of sexual immorality.

YOUR BUSINESS WOULD UNDER PERFORM IF SEXUAL IMMORALITY IS PREVALENT

No matter the investment in your business, no matter the height you have gotten to, no matter the training you give to your staff, if sexual immorality prevails among your management team, your business would die. This is because, very soon, most of your staff would be those that are not competent. Open your eyes and see how many great businesses and individuals have been wrecked by this evil. As you consider your management team, I hope you are not involved? If you are, be very sure that you are in active partnership with your business assassins!

Take note of this and register it at the back of your mind, that in the handling of your business, you mustn't be beclouded by sentiments. So, part ways with the killer manager(s), no matter the number of years you have been together. If they would not embrace change, then do well to save your business at the expense of losing them. If you don't you would eventually lose your business! But mind you, killer managers are more inconsiderate; be rest assured that, if your business eventually dies, they will abandon you and move ahead with their life. They will always do, because at your expense, they have enriched themselves. Even if they did not, they have the credentials and so would naturally move on to other endeavours. So, rescue your business from the hands of the killer managers.

Chapter Twelve: The Killer Product(s)

Your products are the goods you render, either to your customers, partners, associates, or yourself (your business). Your products also include members of staff, because they are part of your business. They reflect any good or service provided by your business.

One thing to note is that, most of your customers, or most people that would patronized your business perceive, or judge the kind of goods, or services you render, when they come in contact with your staff. You need to get this clear. This is because, a lot of businesses with sound backgrounds are failing, not because the goods, or services they offer to the consuming public are bad, but because they neglected the key "goods" – the staff – that eventually, go on to portray their goods and services in bad light.

There is this story about a man who had an encounter with the staff of a business concern. He was a man who believed that, for every good service rendered, deserved a good payment. This was a man, who would go to any length to secure his health. He had health challenge, and had to go to the closest hospital to him, which a friend had recommended to him. He had headed to the hospital, with the belief that the best medical attention and treatment would be offered him. Ironically, his expectations were disappointed by the nurse who attended to him. He had explained his health status to the nurse and how he needed urgent attention, and the following dialogue ensued:

"The doctor is not on seat," the nurse retorted.

"So, when would he be available?: The man queried.

"I don't know," The nurse said.

You can guess how disturbed the man was. It was such that he forgot about his illness, and began to wonder what manner of hospital his friend had recommended to him. Mind you, the hospital was a high profile one in that locality. However, service had been ill-provided by the contact nurse. As he narrated his encounter with his friend, the man vowed to never return to that hospital in his lifetime! He went further to say that he would never refer anybody to that hospital, no matter the need.

Now, imagine the spate of loss customer care could cost a good business with a good owner. But the good owner probably failed to monitor the services rendered by his staff. It grieved me, so much that, when I heard this story, I had told myself that such hospital was not worth being patronized! Mind you, I took this decision after hearing the story, which erased my earlier impression and knowledge of the hospital. Your goods and services, no matter their content, if wrongly delivered, would affect your business negatively. If this continues unchecked, your business is at the verge of collapse.

Few days ago, my thought was interrupted by my mum, who had screamed in the living room. She was reading a newspaper, in the course of which she had stumbled on a report, on a well known brand of carbonated soft drink. The report had it that a customer saw some strange substance in the bottled drink. No one knew how the substance got into the bottle. However, the reporter's intention was to warn people about the product. In fact they had tagged it: **"A killer in the bottle."** The report was to warn people about the brand.

"Please avoid that drink o!" my mother warned everyone that cared to listen. Mind you, this was a good brand and a seasoned product. No matter the name that brand had carved out for itself, you obviously won't be comfortable ordering for such, after getting such information. This is the outcome – such information would not only keep you off such a product, it may also scare you from similar brands. You can imagine ordering a bottled drink and all you do the first few seconds, is to examine the content! You sure would not enjoy the drink.

One thing you need to realize is that, people patronize a product that they have confidence in. Mind you, a slight defect in that product could alter their impression of that product.

A SINGLE DEFECT IN A PRODUCT COULD ALTER PEOPLE'S PERCEPTION OF A GOOD PRODUCT

You don't wait to go to a restaurant and all you do on your meal is to sort out unwanted substance. Of course, you would not enjoy the meal.

As a child, I was allergic to beans. It was not because there was anything bad about beans. It was because, anytime I was served beans, I got the impression that the cotyledons I saw in the beans were tiny worms. By reason of this, the first thing I did was to start sorting out the cotyledons. You can imagine what a task that was! You know what; I found out that a spoonful of beans contained more cotyledons than beans! So by the time I finished sorting out the cotyledons, I found out that I still felt the cotyledons in my mouth as I munched a spoonful! It was so bad that, I would end up throwing up. There was nothing my mother didn't do, to help me see differently. She tried to convince me that, the cotyledons were nutritious. However, her explanations were not convincing to me. I continued this into my adolescent years, when I eventually outgrew my allergy for beans.

This is where I am headed – the cotyledon is a very minute part of a bean, which requires considerable effort to spot and remove. So, it is with a latent defect in a product. It can mar the rest of your products; no matter how good they may be, there is therefore, need to examine some of the killer characteristics a product may have.

Characteristics of a Killer Product
1. **One Year Warranty or Guaranteed Repairs:**
    When you enter some retail shops, you would find products with warrantees. Interestingly, everybody wants to buy products with such warranties, but nobody, in the real sense, wants to buy a product that they would have to return after a few days, weeks or months after purchase, despite the warranty on it.

EVERYBODY LIKES WARRANTIES BUT NOBODY WANTS TO BUYS A PRODUCT THAT WOULD BE RETURNED, DUE TO DEFECTS

We buy products with warranties, not because of the warranties, but because of the peace of mind the thought that we could return the products should they be found to be defective, within stipulated period allowed. This is the point; it is great that your product is coming with a warranty, but if you have a product that is regularly returned within the warranty period, that is a sign of a killer product. You may need to withdraw it from the market. Failure to do that may ultimately affect people's perception of any other products from that organization.

So many businesses have been grounded from the very inception because their owners failed to appreciate the consequences of keeping a bad product in the marketplace. Consequently, they lost their brand as well as their customers.

Let's look at it from another perspective. Assuming you bought a particular brand of electronics and afterwards, it turned out a case of shuttling between the manufacturer's office and your home, to have the appliance repaired instead of enjoying the product, what would be your impression or perception of the manufacturers or of that product? It's only natural that if you have had such experience before, that anytime you enter a shop you don't go near any product that has the logo of that organization. Before you know it, you have transferred such resentment to friends and relations, who may further transfer such feeling to others. What happens afterwards is that such an organization is blacklisted in the minds of people.

Mind you, such blacklisting resulted from the experience the customer had when he purchased one of the organization's defective products. This eventually negatively impact on their other products. Please, note that, the organization may have other good products; nonetheless, one faulty product purchased by a customer is capable of painting every other product manufactured by the organization as inferior or faulty. So you need to take out time to examine how often your warranty programme is put to work. It may be sending you a signal, that you have a killer product trailing your business.

2. The Stain on a White Garment:

In Christianity, a stain on one's garment, which typifies sin is capable of making one miss the chance to enter into the bliss of heaven, and also powerful enough to plunge one into eternal damnation. So it is when we fail to tackle a defect in our products. Like the story I narrated earlier on, about the warning my mother issued about a particular bottled drink, an impression such as this could significantly affect business prospects. You need to thoroughly scrutinize your products before sending them out to the consuming public. The reason for this is that you may not be able to prevent the impact of a single defect, once the product is out there in the public domain. What you must realize is that no matter how white a garment may be, if a single spot is found on it, that single spot is capable of rendering the garment unfit for an outing.

You already know how it feels like when you want to put on your cloths only for you to discover dirt or stain on it. That discovery alone is capable of making you decide not to wear it. You know what; even if you do, your mind will not be at rest. So it is when you take a defective product to the marketplace. The implication is that you reduce the trust and confidence people have in your product!

A DEFFECTIVE PRODUCT REDUCES THE TRUST AND CONFIDENCE OF YOUR CUSTOMERS ON YOUR PRODUCT

This defect may be odour in your restaurant. That is a defect. You may cook the best of meals, but if the environment is stinking, you may be surprised that people may not patronize you. There is a grave consequence, when defective products are sold.

3.   The User-Unfriendly Products:

I still remember the experience I had when my daughter was born. For some reasons, I hadn't purchased my baby's crib on time. So there was a rush when my daughter was brought home from the hospital. I eventually bought one and we hurriedly undid the packaging housing the crib, thinking, the process would be easy. It turned out that we were mistaken! We encountered problems in the process. For one, it turned out that the manual that came with the product was so disorganized that we could not figure out the relationship between the instruction given, as regards the installation of the crib, and the crib itself!

Out of frustration, we had to call the seller. The seller then, called an installer, whom we had to wait for, for eternity! When he eventually showed up, he fixed the crib within a few minutes, what several people had tried to fix for several hours.

That experience was not palatable at all. When I recall the ease with which the installer concluded the setting up of the crib, I wondered why the manufacturers had not properly illustrated that in the manual that came with the crib. And do you know what I eventually gathered? The product that was meant to be user-friendly became one that required an experienced installer! In other words, you would an installer any time you purchase it. The manual was so badly written that, any one that buys the product would have no choice but request for an installer! The aforementioned product, though portrayed as one that is user friendly, was far from meeting that specification!

This is where we are heading; you need to examine your product which you tag as user-friendly, if actually it meets that claim. So then, it is worthy of note, that, just like the crib I purchased, a lot of products are out there in the market, wasting away because their manufacturers are ignorant of the fact that, the so-called user-friendly products are actually chasing away their customers.

The questions you need to ask yourself at this stage are:

i. **Are the goods and services which I claim to be user-friendly actually user friendly?**
ii. **Are the members of staff I project as customer-friendly, meeting that claim?**
iii. **Are my claims of what my business is, meeting that standard?**

What you should guide against is that, if you have a product that needs a manual to assist the final purchaser install its components, you must be very sure that the manual can accomplish the purpose intended. If a customer would need an interpreter, or an expert to install that product, then that must be made very clear, instead of creating a false impression. Mind you, we had to pay the installer extra money to install the crib that was tagged user-friendly – a product that was meant to be installed without the need for an expert.

I don't know if I would discourage anybody from buying that particular brand of crib, but one thing I know is that I would not buy such a product, no matter how urgent it is needed! Till date, I still look at that crib with resentment. And mind you, the crib is a good product, but the installation is not user-friendly.

DON'T CLAIM TO BE WHAT YOU ARE NOT. DON'T PORTRAY YOUR PRODUCTS FALSELY OTHERWISE YOUR GAIN MAY BE ONE OFF AND YOUR LOSS A CONTINUUM.

4. The Product that Requires Continuous Explanation/Apology:

I love the word "sorry". If there is one word I use often it is the word "sorry". I hope to one day make a compilation on that word, but how does this relate to the killer product? Yes, it has a lot to do with the killer products. One thing I discovered lately is that, there are a lot of organizations that are always apologizing for rendering the wrong service. They are sorry for the ill behavior of their staff. They are even sorrier for the ill-performance of their product(s).

You have a killer product trailing your business if you do not have a unit to cater for the needs and complaints of customers. The telecoms business is a very good example, in the sense that, one of the most vital units of any telecommunication company is the customer care unit. This unit is so important because of the nature of the business. This means that, for your business to do well there is the need for it to have a place that caters for the numerous needs and complaints of subscribers.

You have killer products, if at every point in time; you are either apologizing for ill-performance or giving out instructions and explanations on the functionality, operations, workability and installation of the product. I wonder what kind of product that may be, if your customers cannot buy your product and have rest of mind. Is your product one you have to keep defending, or explaining the cause of one defect or another? If that is the case, then you have a killer product trailing your business. You may soon lose your customers and also your **business.**

5. The Under-Performing Product:

Are you in a business with other competitors? If that is the case, you need to be sure your product is not underperforming relative to others.

Are you in a restaurant business? While you wish for customers, your competitors are working hard to accommodate theirs? You need to upgrade your services above their level. It might just be that there is something you are not doing right. I recommend you visit their restaurant, eat their food, speak with their staff, and you might be surprised to find the solution to that problem.

There is no reason someone somewhere is doing well on a product that has become a burden to you. It means that, what you have is underperforming. You need to step it up to the level of performance. Take to the advice given above. Seek and find the secret from your competitors.

SEEK AND FIND THE SECRET WAY YOUR COMPETITORS ARE DOING WELL AND YOU MAY NEED ADJUSTMENTS IN YOUR BUSINESS

Finally, your product should meet the intended purpose. If it does not, put it aside before it kills your business. And mind you, this product could be:

(a) Goods or services.
(b) You or your staff.

So use the parameters given to examine where your business is at the moment, and do the needful. And remember, it is your business. If it is drowning, it will drag you along.

IT IS YOUR BUSINESS, IF IT IS DROWNING, IT WILL DRAG YOU ALONG

Chapter Thirteen: The Killing Effects of Greed and Covetousness

There is a man that has one word in his dictionary – "me". In his vocabulary is the word "me". In his daily life it is "me", and this same man's business is centered on "him". It is almost impossible to divorce oneself from his business. This is because he is the owner of the business – he established it. Fine, your business has been established and it is a success, with sustainability and profit in view, right?

These powerful forces drive most businesses - success, sustainability and profitability. Ironically, in the midst of these forces, two unlikely ills may thrive – **GREED and COVETOUSNESS!**

Mind you. An average man is selfish, greedy and covetous. You may wonder how true this statement is. The answer is simple: Why are you reading this book? Let's say for knowledge and enlightenment. The next question is: This quest is for whom? You, of course! Now, you see, you don't wait until your business dies before you try to rescue it. And mind you, some of your allies may have their own business, but one thing is paramount in this your quest – "self" and "my" business.

This analogy describes the greed in your quest, herein is the puzzle – your quest for knowledge is a type of greed. You want to know more and if the opportunity avails itself, you would prefer to be the first to know and the only one that knows! The unfortunate thing about this is that, life is a bulk of liberality. What we must realize is that, what we may consider as the highest attainment of knowledge; as far as we are concerned, could actually be the beginning of another's.

How about covetousness? Of course there is no man on earth that can claim not to have coveted what another has. You know how often you wondered how you would have felt like if you were the president, or a particular inventor, or the best student! And even now, don't you wish your business won the best business of the year award? That is covetousness in its different guises. As a matter of fact, the list is endless! As seemingly bad as the words "greed and covetous" are, they have their positive sides. Primarily, this has to do with a wish that is not targeted at hurting another, but a desire to be like another, without necessarily harming the person.

Less, there be a twist on the actual meaning of these words, I would prefer to leave them where they actually belong. Indeed, they are interpreted to mean two of life's evils. No matter, how one tries to twist it, as I have tried to do here; to be greedy and covetous is bad and unhealthy. These dispositions have destroyed individuals; have wrecked families, and sent lots of people to their untimely graves.

In my book *Why Students Fail and Spend Extra Years in School*, I did observe that children fail and spend extra year in crèche because of greed and covetousness:

"Greed is an act of desiring what others have above what you have; it does not matter if what you have is better, covetousness sets in, breeding an art of discontent."

The aforementioned has not helped most businesses in any way. Today greed and covetousness have been replaced with terms, like: "diversity" and "globalization" in the business world. All too often, we find that just because company A is doing well trading in bottled water, company B feels it would boost its image to invest in that business area. The far-reaching implications are felt around us. As companies divert from their primary trade to others, where they have little knowledge and experience, even comparative advantage, their main business begins a downward slide. Instead of arresting the slide, they take consolation in the fact that, they are still making profit. But their primary aim of setting up that business far transcends profit making. Interestingly, there is also the issue of sustainability, which most organizations have neglected, in their pursuit of gains.

It is worthy of note that, few businesses have treaded that path. Some have lost their flavour, as a result of such diversion. For those that succeeded, the "greed and covetous" factors may have been reduced to zero. Their diversion may have been out of a sincere desire for growth, not necessarily because another company is profiting from it.

It needs be said that, greed blinds, and that covetousness thrives in blindness. A drive anchored on greed, takes nothing into consideration, save profit (gains). And while covetousness sees nothing, but profit (gains), you can imagine a business decision that is, driven by these two forces. One is blind to everything, except the profit while the other sees nothing, but the profit. I would make this bold declaration at this point:

the fall of many great businesses, nations and empires were as a result of greed and covetousness.

The impact of greed and covetousness does not only apply to existing businesses. It also applies to new ones also. I need to sound a note of warning at this juncture, while also exposing some hidden traits of this evil.

Warnings and Traits of Greed and Covetousness
1)   **Warning:** You need to note and heed the following. Most of the decision a man would make, as long as he is alive, would first be borne out of selfishness, greed and covetousness. A lot of us may not know how these came about, because they do not align with thought or reason but to 'common' sense.

Selfishness, greed and covetousness thrive based on our senses (feeling of attainment and success). They do not align with reason, especially, when the drive is aimed at attaining gain and profit.

2)   **Traits:** Do you make mistakes before you realize that you should have done it differently? You are a victim of greed and covetousness. Continuous regrets on decisions made are traits of greed and covetousness.

Are you easily swayed by gains and profit, without taking into consideration the source or path to such? Then greed and covetousness have taken a hold of you.

Do you see only the success and good of another person's business while your eyes are shut to the activities surrounding such? Greed and covetousness dwell in you!

You have been warned, and also, samples of the traits of these evils have been exposed to you. Let`s examine their killer effects on businesses.

The Killer Characteristics of Greed and Covetousness

1.   The Quest for Gains:

Every business establishment has as its background, the quest for gains, but a business founded, based on the exclusive quest for gains, has the symptoms of greed and covetousness. The reason for this is that an exclusive quest for gain, when setting up a business, blinds one's eyes to possible areas that could truncate such gains.

I have seen this trait in lots and lots of restaurants that eventually crumbled. It is a known fact, that the food business is a very lucrative business; in fact there is a ready market for this business. The question is: Why are a lot of restaurants, eateries and canteens folding up, in spite of the ready market?

The answer is as simple as the query. Those restaurants eateries and canteens that failed to succeed were set up under the influence of greed and covetousness.

One thing you must note here is that, unlike pride, greed and covetousness are not easily noticeable, particularly, when it has to do with business decisions. No marvel then, that, a lot of people who may be reading this segment might argue, rationalizing as follows: What is wrong if a man enters into a business with gains in view? A lot is wrong because such position would not make such a person to make the necessary research and also make reasonable moves.

The sad truth about most businesses that, have folded up is that, they died because of the effects of greed and covetousness. Mind you, an average man as earlier stated is both greedy and covetous, and when these traits, overwhelm one in ones business decisions, a lot of wrong choices would be made. No marvel then, that, most businesses that were borne out of the drive for gains and profitability soon went under.

This does not only apply to businesses; it applies to our day to day lives, as well. Consider the case of most of the school drop-outs we have in our midst, today; a lot of them, enrolled for a particular course of study, because of the gains in view, while failing to take into consideration, the cost implications, as well as, their natural bent. So, you find them falling by the way side, from their medical courses, engineering and so on.

ANY ENTRANT INTO ANY BUSINESS BORNE SOLELY OUT OF GAINS, WOULD AMOUNT TO A GREAT LOSS, BECAUSE SUCH A BUSINESS – LIKE OTHERS OF ITS KIND - WOULD DIE.

2. The Quest for Supremacy:

More men have been humiliated by their quest for supremacy, which is often interpreted as more wealth, relative to others. I cannot but recall a story in *Acres of Diamond* by Richard Conwell. In that story, a man sold all he had, for what he did not have, and ended up with nothing, save death by suicide.

The quest for supremacy would not only have been occasioned by pride, but by greed and covetousness - a system that prompts you to create a non-existing competition, so that you start a battle with yourself. To you, it might be with your competitors. No marvel you delve into all sorts of sponsorships and programs — all aimed at proving your wit. In so doing, you have failed to realize that you are spending more and realizing close to nothing, in return.

Your quest for supremacy has blinded you. Your greed and covetousness, and strive to surpass your competitors has driven you to their line of business. No marvel, your war with them has turned out to be their gain, because your product cannot compete with theirs. By venturing into that line of business that, they have comparative advantage, you have, unknowingly helped to highlight the superiority of their product.

Greed and covetousness have plunged a lot of businesses into some harsh realities. They may even think that, all the necessary steps have been taken but alas, one thing they may have failed to realize is that, greed and covetousness, blind man to reason, and that, some things are simply not unrealistic.

YOU CANNOT DO WHAT AND ALL IT TAKES IN A LINE OF BUSINESS, WHEN YOU ARE UNDER THE INFLUENCE OF GREED AND COVETOUSNESS.

Your quest for supremacy is driven by greed and covetousness. It is worthy of note that, no business thrives under such alliance.

3. Divided Attention:

Some light has earlier been shed on this, to buttress; greed and covetousness make a business owner have divided attention. It is worthy of note that, an investor should keep his ears to the ground and his eyes wide open, so as to tap into some profitable ventures. It should however be done outside the influence of greed and covetousness.

An attention divided, investment-wise would plunge a business into inconclusive transactions. Such a business may well have its eyes wide open and its ears to the ground, but the outcome of such outlook is that, such a business owner may take time, to enter into any business that seems to be making waves. In so doing, things that should be considered deeply are omitted. No marvel, therefore, that such a business oscillates between gains and losses – avoidable losses, at that.

Recently I came across two different business owners. In each instance, either was asked the nature of their business and these were their responses:

Business man A: "Here is my card, I'm into real estate. I am also into catering, electrical works…. In fact I can do anything".

Hang on to this response, as we consider the response of business man B.

Business man B: "I have worked for several organizations. I worked as a marketer with a construction company. For now I can Market anything, but am also a good caterer……."

Something I wish to reveal about these two persons is that their businesses seem not to be doing well. The realization that struck me was that their businesses were operating under divided attention. In fact, at a point I had to advise both that, with their approach to their businesses, they would be losing much of their prospective customers. I made both of them to realize that when you have a prospective client, the client's interest should first and foremost be considered before you start telling the client that you can do virtually every and anything. And of course, you and I know that, there is no business in the world that is so easy that a person that wants to be very competent in it can afford to give it divided attention. Moreover, no prudent person would want to interact with such a business that is claiming to be capable of carrying out all activities.

The advice is that, if the prospective client is interested in catering, it is better to talk more about your business proficiency in catering rather than, the claim to be jack of all trades. No marvel that, from my perception their businesses are far from doing well.

Recently, I was on a business trip to seal a deal for my organization, centered on acquisition of property. Unfortunately for us, that line of business was no longer available. So, our client told us, of the likelihood of taking up the construction of towers. I quickly made it clear to them that, we are not involved with construction of towers. Mind you, as at the time of that meeting, my organization could actually handle the offer, but we realized that accepting the offer, far from portray us in a good light, before our client, and it may create a wrong impression about our organization.

Here is the core of the matter – businesses are being killed because of the inability to control greed and covetousness. The other vice is, divided attention. Stick to simplicity. Do all the necessary analysis and don't just accept an offer because others are doing well in it, or because of gains. The watchword is focus, and plan before diversification.

Chapter Nineteen: Impacts of Health, Safety and Welfare (HSW)

In the analysis of the killer structure, and the business environment, part of H.S.E was analyzed. So what we have here is H.S.W – health, safety and welfare. I would like to start this analysis with a quote from Richard Templar, culled from his book: *The Rules of Management*, on the role of a manager:

"The role of a manager is to manage processes rather than people. People can manage themselves if you let them".

I would like to extract two phrases from the aforementioned. The first is: "The role of the manager is to manage processes", and the second is: "People can manage themselves". For some personal reasons, I wish to state that, I just read that, passage of his book and the words struck my heart real hard –this is exactly why it appeared on this passage on HSW.

A business is a component of two parts – the process and the people. If you critically examine the processes of a business, their successes are, to a large extent, dependent on H.S.W. The component of people relies on H.S.W. Health, safety and welfare (H.S.W) will keep both your business processes and the human components at high performance; provided they are adequate, and high levels of concern are directed at them.

It is worthy of note that, most organizations are very critical about the Health, Safety and Environment of their business, while quite a number of organizations neglect them. Included also, in H.S.E are issues that have to do with welfare. For purpose of clarity, welfare should not be viewed only from the angle of humans, but also from the processes of the business, which includes tools, machineries, buildings and other physical structure that requires much care.

How would you position your business? Progressing, thriving, ailing, dying, or dead? If you are not clear on the location (status) of your business, it is indicative that, your business may be ailing. This is because, inability to define your business status is a major indicator that, it is ailing However, if your business status is undefined, or you are convinced that your business is failing and you have done all your analysis, and the findings are inconclusive, on the source of the failure, then you may need to examine the H.S.W of your business.

I would have you know that, more and more businesses are ailing, unknown to the owners because of their failings in the areas of HSW. You see, HSW cuts across all components of your business – your good self inclusive! How? Let's extract health for a start. There is the saying that: "A sick man cannot reason properly". Now imagine, a business discussions that emanate from one so characterized (a person that is ill), what do you expect?

Now, bring this to yourself. Assuming, you are that type of entrepreneur that finalizes on actions to be taken, and it happens that, at the same time, your health is failing. What do you think would happen to your business? Now, imagine also that your workforce health status is not taken into consideration, and all your organization is interested in, is that, their job is done, what kind of product, or output do you expect would be produced? Do also, consider a situation, where there is no health provision for your staff, and yet you expect them to perform. Such an expectation is deceitful, and would crumble any business.

Let's consider the safety aspects of your business. It is rather sad, to note, that, lots of manufacturing businesses are embroiled in litigations, arising from negligence on their part, as far as safety is concerned. There are industries, where labourers are made to work under severe and dangerous conditions. One thing, you should realize, is that, any organization operating under such conditions is not only ailing, but dead.

What about welfare, are you not neglecting your staff welfare? Your business output is directly proportional to your staff welfare. And your staff performance is a reflection of your welfare package.

The words: "I don't care" must be removed from your vocabulary, as far as your staff welfare is concerned. And of course, why should you not care, now, after you have engaged your staff? If you would recall, one major criterion, used during your staff selection, was their health status, so we can say, that, you engaged them, because they were healthy. Now, you don't seem to care again about their health status. That need, not only to be preserved; but must be improved upon, and the sure way to do that, is through workable welfare policy. You have to "care" from this moment onwards about the health of the staff in your organization if you want to rescue your business from underperformance or improve its level of performance.

Recently, I had a discussion with a staff who complained of headache. From the look on her face, I could see the distress she was going through. This reflected in the way, she carried out her job. Look here, you don't want your customer/client confronted by a sick staff. What kind of impression are you creating?

So what do we have here? Simple:

Health + safety = welfare.

If so:

$HSW = (Health + safety)(Health + safety) = (Health + safety)^2$.

The mathematical representation clearly shows that, to keep your business on top, you need more than just a thorough health and safety policy; you need to multiply it for effectiveness. If at present, your output is dwindling, you can review it by doubling your staff welfare package.

I have been to an organization, where most of the time, staff are busy complaining, neglecting their jobs. And what are they complaining about? Welfare! And what is the management doing about that? Nothing! What is the result? Of cause, staffs working with their heads, and not with their heart or mind. So you have people in your organization, who are not necessarily working for you!

Welfare plus welfare is a necessary component for business growth, so, don't ignore it, if you want profit and sustainability. You can actually get people to work for you till death, once they are convinced that you are interested in their health, safety and welfare. When you have these kinds of people, you have what is referred to, in chemistry, as "ionic bond" – a type of bond that requires a lot of fire and heat to disintegrate. You have a group of people, bonded together as a team; willing not only, to protect your business by their deliverables, but also their H.S.W, because they know that, the better their output, the better their H.S.W. However, if their case is on the contrary, they would most likely, treat your business as they would treat their waste.

Let's quickly examine the behaviour of the killer H.S.W.

Characteristics of the Killer H.S.W

1. Your Business Stinks to Your Staff:

Do you know that, as you have bad odour and unsavoury taste in meals, so also you have with businesses? A business that treats the H.S.W of its staffs as unimportant would be stinking to the staffs. Let me pause here, and ask you a question: Have you ever entered a toilet that stinks? Did you endure the smell while you used it? Did you flee? Personally, I don't waste time in such a place. I take to my heels. So, what could be done to make such a toilet fit for use? First, the toilet would have to be flushed and cleaned properly. But remember that the stench would still remain. However, there is a remedy for that – the application of air freshener to subdue the stench.

Your business is like a toilet that stinks, if you reject the H.S.W of your staff, and like my attitude towards a toilet that stinks, you are more likely to lose your staff to your competitors for the simple fact that, nobody likes a foul odour.

I know a young man who once worked for a firm. Because of the poor H.S.W of the firm, the first thing he did, when he reported to work was to pray that God should deliver him from the company. If this young man forgot anything at all, he certainly never forgot to pray, upon resumption, since it was now apparent that, the work had become irritating to him.

Let's analyze this kind of behavior. Mind you, it was not only the young man that was working with that organization that was, displeased with the company's policy on H.S.W. Other members of staff were displeased, as well. At one time, this young man, and most of his contemporaries in that organization, left the firm. To the young man, working with that organization was hell.

You need look beyond your toilet. You need to examine the stench your business is emitting. The provision you have made, as far as H.S.W is concerned, is negatively reflecting on your staff's behavior.

You need to realize that, when people who are working for you are wishing and praying that they would have the opportunity to exit the firm, instead of wishing, or praying for the wellbeing of your business, they are indeed expressing their unhappiness with the state of affairs in your organization. It is therefore, no marvel that, you always have to repeat instructions and that your managers have to shout; command and sometimes, almost go physical, to be able to implement an action. All these, are a waste of resources. Your business is now stinking, as far as members of staff are concerned. You need to examine your H.S.W.

2. The Complaining Staff:

Is your business output stagnant? One complains of his health, another of the risk involved in your business and yet you have failed to listen. These are signs that you have neglected their welfare and also the state of the tools used in your business. Let me shout this out to your hearing:

YOUR BUSINESS WOULD SOON DIE, IF YOU ARE BLIND TO THE WELFARE OF YOUR STAFF!

How do I know that my H.S.W is not effective? You ask. The answer is hidden in your staff complaints. Listen to their complaint. Recently, a C.E.O assembled his members of staff, and the message to them was clear:

"IF YOU ARE NOT MAKING ENOUGH FROM THIS JOB, THAT MEANS I HAVE FAILED – MY ADVICE TO EACH AND EVERYONE ONE OF YOU IS THAT, YOU QUIT THE JOB."

This was a declaration. You can guess the outcome. None of the staff quitted, but rather they intensified their effort and the outcome was tremendous.

Now, there are some things I wish you would covet and that is, the attitude of the CEO, in as much as I am against covetousness, I would advise you to covet this one, so that you can improve your business output via an improved H.S.W. Your staff should not be the complaining type. They should zealously work in tandem with your vision. But a vision that is, tied only to your joy; at the expense of theirs, would only breed dissatisfied and complaints. This would negatively impact on your business, in the long run.

3.   "This is Hell!" – Does this Phrase Describe Your Business?

Hell? What a way, to describe a business! Of course you are responsible for that title, you and your staff, could so describe your business to the hearing of others. The truth is that, when members of staff, work in an un-conducive environment, they come away feeling used. You have turned your business into hell. If your staff are losing their limbs, or arms; their breathing is impaled; their sight is being affected by reason of the activities being carried out in your organization. It implies that, their wages are being returned into your business, when they spend it all, treating themselves of ailments, or deformity incurred in the course of working in your organization. In some cases, you may have used your business to put asunder, some families, because of the unhealthy work schedule. So, what do you have here? A hell of business! You don't care about what happens to the H.S.W of your staff, and because of that, your staff now term working for you as hell. So, what output do you expect from them? Zero!

There have been factories where people are forced to work under unhealthy and inhuman conditions. Some, knowing full well that, their actions are criminal, subdue their staff and force them to work. Some, even, go as far, as trafficking unskilled laborers to work under such severe conditions. These kinds of cases abound. We have reports of factories, with poor, or inadequate safety provisions. When some of the victims of the factory owners' negligence are interviewed, they tend to give an account that best describe the factories as hell, and a place, unfit to work.

Note, this fact, if your business is on this path, it is obvious that, what you consider to be profits are actually loses. This is, because, one day, your business would either die naturally, or the authorities will shut it down.

4.   Interest in Healthy Employees Versus Neglect of Health Of Employees:

Is your business, so characterized? Are you only interested in employing only healthy people, without putting in place a welfare package that, will sustain their health? You need to honestly answer this question yourself, by examining your welfare package. In doing this, you have to tie your welfare package to your choice criteria. How to do this is simple – your choice of an employee was tied, not only to his skills, but his health, right? However, have you put in place, what would not, only, sustain this health, but what would improve it?

At this juncture, I know your mind would flash to the health centres, and first aid that have been made available. Good. But even, if all these things are in place, H.S.W still transcends these. It rests more, on the overall packages like:

-        Payment for overtime
-        Provision of work gadgets
-        A conducive Work environment
-        Vacations
-        Allowances etc.

Hey, if members of staff are not happy and are complaining, then, this attitude will negatively affect your business. If your business, seems not to be progressing at your desired pace, the secret is for you to look at the above list, to see the areas where your organization hasn't done much. Note, that, a good H.S.W, would keep your staff physically refreshed, and mentally and emotionally alert, and healthy. But it must also be noted, that, while some organizations cater for the physical health of their staff, they neglect their emotional and mental health. How?

The neglect of staff training, is mental health neglect. What indicates this is lack of staff training. Your behavior is comparable to the farmer that regularly milks the cow without feeding it appropriately. What you should note here, is that, there is almost nothing in nature that, is permanent. We have seen cases of animals like, the dinosaurs that went extinct. There is also the forecast that, should man continually extract crude oil from the earth crust, that very soon, we would run out of oil. No marvel then, that, the world is presently exploring other sources of energy.

AN EMPLOYER THAT NEGLECTS STAFF TRAINING IS JUST LIKE A FARMER THAT REGULARLY MILKS HIS COW WITHOUT COMMENSURATE FEEDING

You may wonder where this analysis is heading. You need not wonder too much. It is aimed at the neglect of staff training, and that, by implication is that, you would soon drain out the zeal of your staff, leading to monotony and low, or no creativity. The reason is not far-fetched – your organization's staff can only do what they are used to, because staff training has been neglected. The impact is low productivity.

The aforementioned could also lead to emotional distortion of the staff. You have decided to use your business to frustrate your staff that may result in the loss of "love and affection" between them and the people they love. Gone are the days when workers were treated like slaves or made to work round the clock like modern day computers based on the thinking that, all you need to do, was issue the command and press the right buttons. Take note that, members of your staff have choices. They have feelings just like you do. You should not trample on their emotions. If you do, the implication would be dire, particularly, on your business.

Don't you see failure, when the countenance of your staff depicts frustration – a sign that buttresses lack of H.S.W (sorry, appropriate H.S.W)? Obviously, this is a by-product of the unilateral direction of your interest in the health of your business, and the neglect of the health of your staff. Some may have been discussed. Maybe, you think that you are not guilty of the above-mentioned issues, but are you guilty of neglecting your staff FINANCIAL HEALTH?

What kind of C.E.O are you, if your staff's welfare – particularly their financial health – is missing as far as your priorities are concerned. But mind you, if you neglect their financial health, they may likely steal from you, at the slightest opportunity. What you should note, is that, this century has witnessed so much financial fraud in the corporate world, a trend which has become quite alarming.

Here you are now, and I wish to make it clear that, I would be winding up on this segment with this very issue that led to the setting up of most businesses – "finance". Recall one of your major drives, was financial liberation. Now, let me ask you this question: **What do you think, made your employee decide to work with you? Don't you think it all boils down to financial liberation?**

If the aforementioned is accurate, you need to treat them as you would treat your business. By having financial gains and libration in view, you already know what neglect of your core interest (finances) in your business could lead to, so would the neglect of the core interest (finances) of your employee lead to. This neglect could kill your business.

If you don't want to convert loyal employees into financial threats, you need to be interested in their financial welfare. Recently, I met a man, who boldly declared that, the way the company he works for was going, failure was imminent. I was at a loss, at such an outburst especially from a man who had, in the past, spoken well about this same organization. But that interest had been substituted with disinterest and revolt. In fact, he made it known to me that, his current opinion about the organization he works with is not restricted to him alone, but that it cuts across the board. So, what was the problem? I wanted to know. The answer was simple – the organization he works with had decided to embrace shambles. Staff welfare was neglected. At the fore of this neglect, was their financial health. The organization had decided to toe the part of creating disharmony among staff. How? I asked. Here is his reply, in his exact words:

"When you now have to report to a subordinate; I mean a person, not as qualified as you are, being promoted above you. You can imagine such, not only earning much more than you but giving you orders".

I felt for this young man. His case was similar to what I had experienced in the past. These were cases that clearly shows neglect of a staff's financial heath – a situation where proper financial obligation are thrown to the winds; where the proprietor doesn't want to reason, even when that business is seating on a very potent killer – neglect of H.S.W. I don't know how proper this quote "the ball is on your court" is, but I would round up with a little twist to that quote:

THIS BUSINESS YOU HAVE SET UP IS IN YOUR COURT. ON THE OTHER COURT (YOUR OPPONENT'S) AND EVEN IN YOUR'S ARE THE KILLERS.

Remember, it is your business. If it eventually drowns, it will drag you along. I hope you will protect your business from these killers.

PART 3: BUSINESS KILLERS IN ACTION

INSIGHT

There is a mantra that goes thus: "There is no"smoke without fire."
What that statement means, is that, smoke comes after fire; smoke
is the aftermath of fire, smoke trails fire. What you have read so
far, are "fires". What you shall be reading next are "smokes".

"Smokes" usually do not stay with their host. If you are some
distance away from the fire, you may not notice the flame, what
you would see are smokes. Sometimes, these smokes may journey
very far from their sources that, if care is not taken, you may not be
able to trace them to their origin. So, is the work of business killers,
these killers are the flame, or fire that burns the business. What you
see is smokes that soars so high, and eventually disappears.

Before delving further on this analysis, let's consider some of the
characteristics of smokes:

1. They trail fire.
2. They can travel as far as the wind carries them.
3. They can soar as high as possible until they disappear
4. Smokes determine the end of a fire.
5. Smokes are like spirit that leaves a dying man. What is left
    behind is the deceased's corpse.
6. Smokes are like mirage. You see them and after a while they
    are no more. They leave behind sorrow.
7. Smokes chokes and kills because there is no life in it.
8. Smokes are signs of bad omen. They arouse fear and alert
    that there is chaos somewhere.
9. When you see smokes, the first thing that comes to your
    mind, is trouble.
10. Finally, smoke, when inhaled by choice, still spells danger –
    "….smoking is dangerous to your health".

Now let's relate these characteristics to the business world. You
would recall, what we said about fire and smoke. Fire was referred

189

to as the business killer, while smoke is a sign of a dying business. Let's relate these characteristics to a dying business.

1. **Smokes trail fire:** When a business is under attack by business killers, a lot of negative things begin to happen, the business begins to ail, outputs and profit falls – though gradually – but the signs are always evident.

2. **Smokes can travel as far as the wind can carry it:** When this is related to an ailing business, it is referring to activities that may still be going on in the business. Although such a business may be dying, it may still be in the news. They may be declaring profit, and posting dividends. Mind you what is being displayed is a smoke screen. Life is gradually drifting from the business.

3. **Smokes can soar as high as possible until they disappear:** So it is, with a business that has caved in, to these killers. They may seem to be going higher and higher, because of the profits and dividends being declared. The CEO and the board members of the business may seem to be doing well, but when the true records are opened, such a business may have gone past recovery!

4. **Smokes determine the end of a fire:** A dying business is one that is filled with activities and expenses and yet void of profit. Nothing is actually moving. It is very possible that, where you found the business yesterday is the same place you would still find the business today. This is the signs of the end of the business.

5. **Smoke leaves behind carcasses:** A dead business leaves behind, displeased customers, creditors and frustrated staffs.

These are some of the carcasses that would **be left behind by "business killers".**

6. **Smoke is like mirage:** what you see in a dying business are falsehood – false accounts, false ledgers, false salary payments, false profit declaration. These are things you would not see until you probe deep into the dying business.

7. **Smoke chokes and kills because there is no life in it:** So, it is, with a dying business. Those that, dare do business with such a dying business, might end up been, infested with the problems of such business. People may end up, losing their hard earned money; goods taken, would not be paid for. They may drag those that, deal with them, into unprofitable litigations.

8. **Smoke is a bad omen; it creates signs of chaos:** These are some of the signs the world is presently facing – economic meltdown, which transpired because, that, some jobs were executed badly. Others are suffering the consequences of negligence. More and more businesses are, ailing and dying, because of the failure of some other businesses.

9. **Smoke portrays the occurrence of destruction:** So is a dying business. Smoke cripples a lot of good activities. It is a sign that, things are going bad. It informs of problems, or negligence. It is a sign of collapse. So, when you see such traits of business killers, you know that, the end of such a business is near.

10. **Smoking is dangerous to your health:** That is the warning, we hear each day on the streets, or when we watch our television sets. The adverts are there: "The Federal Ministry

of Health warns that smokers are liable to die young." This is the type of warning smokers in Nigeria and elsewhere get.

The warning I want to give you at this point is that: **YOUR BUSINESS WOULD DIE NOW IF YOU DO NOT COMBAT BUSINESS KILLERS.** The above listed points are illustrations of what you would encounter in this section. You will see how some businesses were killed due to the influx of business killers. You would journey into how some small-scale businesses were assassinated by these killers. Restaurants, schools, banks, manufacturers, and even nations have died due to the impacts of these killers. So brace yourself, for the issues at hand, require your attention. These facts would help prevent your business from falling prey to these killers, or help you rescue your ailing business from the grip of these killers. So then, if your business is dying, you need not stand helplessly looking at it. If your career is dwindling, you need not stand helplessly looking confused. If your world is failing, you need to do something about it so as to checkmate the action of business killers.

Here is your last chance to avenge yourself of these killers. Do not let them escape. The traits of BUSINESS KILLERS IN ACTION have been exposed.

Chapter One: The Killing of Restaurants

A free meal could be very costly in the long run. This was my experience a few years ago. My friend – a very generous one, for that matter – had taken me out for a free meal. The restaurant was neat and well arranged. Our orders were taken and in time, two plates of rice were served us. I observed that, in spite of how beautiful and well kept the restaurant was, it was literally empty. This puzzled me a great deal. My friend immediately pounced on his meal. He must have scooped and swallowed two spoonfuls or more, while I was yet to swallon a spoonful. "Hey, stop there!" I had interrupted my friend from further eating the food. I drew his attention to the slippery state of the rice and the odour, which were signs that the food was stale. It was then he also realized that the rice he had been eating had gone bad.

Our query on why this restaurant, which used to be a fast-moving restaurant gradually, became empty was confirmed. So, we called the attention of the service personnel who also confirmed that the meal was bad. Then, she said: "Let me get you guys a replacement." We were very furious at that statement. We made her realize that it was out of place to serve customers meals they knew had gone stale. Moreover, we made her realize that, she had no conviction that what would be served next would not be bad.

We left the restaurant, with a vow never to return. No wonder the restaurant was losing customers! It was essentially because of the state of food they serve. Not too long, that restaurant wound up. Similarly, many restaurants are winding up operations because their owners paved a way for business killers to set in and destroy their businesses, right, before their very eyes.

The above illustration is a business killed by some of the killers that have been identified in this book. Let`s arrange them one after the other:

i.   **The Owner:** The owner of that business, obviously, must be one that, does not take his time to examine the output of the restaurant. If he did, he would have realized that, his customers were depleting. He would have taken necessary steps to investigate and curb the source of the problem.

    I don't know the owner, but one thing is certain; if the owner was involved in that business, he would have realized that the food he was serving to customers was what was chasing customers away from the business and that, this would kill the business, which was what eventually happened.

ii.   **Staffs:** The business was obviously left in the hands of untrained staffs. If not, what on earth would make them serve customers spoilt meal?

    Mind you, their appearance seemed OK, but that was just a smoke screen. Their activities seemed OK, but the business was dying! Obviously, untrained personnel were actually running the business. And regardless of the spate of activities, the business was dying.

iii.   **Product:** Finally the product of that business – food. Though this is naturally a good product, it was however badly presented. The consequence was that those that had entered the restaurant to eat left, with a vow never to return, even if that restaurant is the only restaurant in the world, that they would rather die of starvation than patronize it! You have seen how a well crafted business, was killed by the owner, his staff and the product. So it is with a lot of restaurants.

It is worthy of note that one business that is most likely to succeed, is the food business. However, this business is a delicate one. Are you into food business? Is your business expressed in the form of restaurants, eateries or fast food? Here are some of the signs that the business might soon fold up, if you do not give it the required attention:

a. Where your customers leave a large chunk of meals uneaten.

b. Where there are regular complaints and confrontations between your staff and customers, due to their behaviour, or the condition of the meal.

c. Where the number of people that, usually visit your restaurant keeps dropping on a daily, weekly, monthly, or yearly basis. You need to assess your business. It may be under the attack of business killers.

In my research, one thing I realized about the food business is that, a lot of those who go into it start the business very well, but continuation is always the problem. This is because, over time, the standard of service begins to drop. One other major cause of this is when such business start to expand and franchises are created with little or no checks and balances in place. In some cases, even though, such checks and balances are contemplated, there are no effective monitoring and enforcement teams put in place.

A friend once told me that he visited a particular fast food restaurant. While there, he noticed that the foot-mat was always unkempt. Worse still, the tables were littered with empty plates and leftovers from customers. At a point, he approached the restaurant manager. Curiously, the restaurant manager shifted the blame to his sub-ordinates! In spite of that, it took the superior some time to effect the clearing of the tables.

My friend made it clear to me that, the reason he kept going there to eat was due to the lack of other options, and also proximity.

Later, something happened that made him resolve to travel the distance, to find a better restaurant.

It happened that one day; he had gone to the restaurant to have his lunch only to find a seal on the entrance, placed there by the food and drink regulatory agency. They had shut down the restaurant as a result of the filthiness of the place. He later found out that a displeased customer had reported that restaurant to the food monitoring agency, which eventually led to the shutting down of the place.

One thing to note is that, a fast food restaurant may be a franchise and thus the strict supervision and control by the original franchise owner may be relaxed. If the fast food business was not operated as a franchise, then it means that the management had failed to carry out its duties. In the process, they lost one of their loyal customers (my friend) and many others – including me! One thing you have to realize is that, the loss of a customer may lead to the loss of many other potential customers. Recall the concluding statement, in chapter 12, of part one: **Your business depends on your structure, keep it working, and KEEP IT CLEAN, Maintenance is management.**

Your restaurant business is in the shadows of death, if the environment in which you operate is not kept clean. Mind you, it may not be shut down by the enforcement agency, but something else, would shut it down – the exit of your loyal customers. And of course, you know that, the lack of customers, means loss of profit and ultimately, the death of the business.

Is your restaurant, which used to bring you lots of profit ailing? If the two illustrations of the action of business killers seem not to have shown you the cause, then you may need to consider the next, hear this tale that is centred on sole-proprietorship. A middle aged woman, who saw a fertile ground to show-case her cooking skills ventured into the food business. The business had started very small, but overtime her business began to expand, so, she moved to a bigger space, employed more hands and also increased her productivity. To her surprise, her expansion could not meet up with the influx of customers, so she expanded her space further. In spite of this, she was confronted with a long queue, notwithstanding the fact that, she had increased her service team. People, in spite of the very long queue, continued to patronize her services. The meal was fantastic. Although, she was surrounded by several competitors, yet they were no match, when it came to what she had to offer. While their restaurants would be empty, customers would queue for meal at the restaurant of this particular woman. Then quite ironically, it happened that she suddenly started losing her customers. The queue began to shrink. Her competitors were now been patronized by some of her very loyal customers. What happened?

The answer to that query was with that woman. She could not manage her success. Initially, she was very much involved with the business, but at some point, she had cut off herself from the business. She was now the cashier and she handed over the business indirectly to untrained hands. This meant that most of those she entrusted her business to, brought their crude and rude behaviour to bear on the business. Arguments became commonplace between staffs and customers – **you remember the analysis on tongues of fire.** How would you manage it (as a customer), when a waiter that ought to be attending to you in the restaurant starts referring you to their competitors? **"Look here, you are not the only customer we have. If you can't wait, or if you are in a hurry, you can go to another place to eat."** Such was the statement a lot of customers received from her staffs. Some endured it, because they loved the meals. Eventually, the meals began to depreciate in quality. The environment became filthy due to neglect, so much so that, customers became largely dissatisfied. Some of her customers started giving the other restaurants a try. They eventually realized that, there was really no big deal, wasting their time queuing up, for food at one restaurant, when there were alternatives. Over time, the queue thinned and the business eventually disappeared with the queue. The business died.

What you should learn from this story is that no matter your clientele base; no matter how fantastic your products may be; if you treat your product and its delivery badly, or if you care less about your customers, that business would eventually die.

Now, don't ever make the mistake of referring your customers to your competitors. In fact, if there is one staff you should immediately sack, it is the staff that does that. You must learn to attend to all your customers the best way possible. If there must be delay (which must be avoided at all cost), then, a thorough explanation (and possibly compensation) should be given the affected customer.

Their love for your product is not a means for you to make yourself indispensable. Mind you, they are probably with you, because of their trust and possibly lack of information, that your competitors are the same, or could do better than you. Your primary duty, as well as that of your staff, should be to keep your customers, by putting things in order, so that, your customers would not be exposed to your competitors. Note the following:

- **Do not displease your customers.**
- **Do not refer them to your competitors.**
- **In fact, talk less about your competitors in the hearing of your customers, or else you would end up, marketing your competitors to them. As for your customers they may end up giving your competitors a trial, and may never return to you!**

Do you have dubious sales personnel who are used to saying: "No change", or "Sorry, I misplaced your receipts" handling your sales? What such attitude would result to is that you will end up with customers that would dread your business and may never return to patronize your business again.

If a customer can afford to pay for a service, it is your duty to give him his balance and receipts; if you do not have his balance, or misplacing his receipt should not be a fault transferred to the customer. In most cases, attributes like this, are intended to induce customers to part with their balance, or cheat them. In some cases, the claim is that, the receipts have been misplaced!

A lot of restaurants are folding up because of these bad traits. Your staffs are undoing your business by chasing away your customers and you seem not to bother. Mind you, what you have is a smoke, and if you understand the analysis on smoke, you would realize that your business venture is already dead and is awaiting its burial. What would happen is that when the revelation of the death of your business would come, it would be sudden because then there would be no remedy. You would have lost all your customers and also the staff that contributed to the death of your business.

You have seen what business killers have done to some restaurants. Are you in the restaurant, eatery or fast food business? Is your business ailing or your profit has, for some time now, been stagnant? You may need to pause and examine your business. It may be under the attack of business killers. The guide to know, if your business is ailing, dying or long dead; you are to use that key to assess your business so that what you have laboured to build would bring you the desired result.

Chapter Two: The Killing of Banks

This era has witnessed the death of more banks than, ever before. Business killers seem to have infiltrated lots of banks. Globally, it is an evil that has bedeviled many countries. What you would get here, is an analysis of the impacts of these killers, though, without any specific reference to any bank, dead, or dying. The reason for this is that, a lot of banks that seem active today are actually "smokes". They are dying, while some are actually dead and decaying. These are the effects of business killers' infiltration. Let's start from the phrase "dead, or alive".

Yes, so many banks are dead. They have been liquidated, while those still running their businesses (even if they are managing or coping) are alive – as long as they have not been liquidated. Indeed, So many factors are responsible for the death of a bank, but specifically let's examine some of those banks that caved in to business killers, how were they killed?

What I want you to realize at this juncture is that, the banking business is one whose cloak of protection is loose, but to on-lookers they seem to be well protected. So, what you often have, are issues of financial misappropriation and fraud. The fact remains that; all businesses could be crumbled by both financial misappropriation and fraud. It is no longer news, when a bank caves in to fraud. Does that mean banks should be left to contend with these evils, as they emerge? Would it not be safer to guard against the infiltration of the sector by business killers?

There is the need for those loose ends to be tied together. These killers need to be exposed. A reference to the analysis on the killing of a restaurant would be a good reference point, to expose business killers relative to banking operations.

Let's recall the reference to the restaurant that, had more customers, than it could manage while there were others close by that, had less patronage. There was something responsible for a reduction in the number of customers that, the favoured restaurant had, which was the quality of food served. But, it is sad to note that the restaurant owner was not concerned about the quality of the food. Apart from that, she hired unqualified staff; got herself out of the mainstream of the business and finally failed to protect her customers. Eventually, the business was killed.

So it would be, with a bank that has failed to protect its customers. The question is: Why would a bank not protect its customers? A lot of reason may be adduced for this:

1.   Bankers to the Government:

A lot of banks that have strong affiliation to the government of a country as far as revenue collection and other forms of concession are concerned; seem to be less concerned about other customers. No marvel, they don't treat other customers with care.

2.   Bankers to Big Time Investors:

Quite a number of banks fall into this category. What is obvious is the unfavorable environment created for small time investors and customers. They over elevate their standards. Let's stop at these two reasons for now. So how do this impact negatively on banks?

It would suffice to note that, in third world countries, or developing countries, the change of government, sometimes, means the change of policy. What you have is that banks, appointed to service a public sector agency stands the chance of losing that service, if there is a change in government. So, what happens? The events are so drastic – signs of distress begin to surface, since such banks have placed their hopes on the government of the day, discarding other customers. Failure may set in, because their key customer has left them.

Let's examine this kind of attitude. Because you have one good customer, you treat others with levity. Maybe, there are holders of such banks who do not know how their customers are treated. It would be ironic to think that the C.E.O does, or staff of the bank does not know that the words: "We don't need your money" could do the bank in, in the near future.

What a way to respond to a customer! Assuming that truly you don't need the money of a 'small time' customer, you have failed to realize that the big time customers you have today were once 'small time' customers. So, what happens when you keep chasing small time investors away; when they eventually grow, your bank would lose potential big time customers that would have had a decision to make, to bank with your bank, as a matter of choice.

Mind you, you might have increased your marketers, rebranded and improve other services. You might eventually, realize that, such, would be in vain because you have already created a wrong impression that yours is a bank that is too big for "small customers". Consequently, they have embraced those that opened their doors to them. Get this clear – people have a right over their money and that right could be used at will. So when you displease a lot of your customers, lots of money may eventually leave your bank.

If your bank is ailing today, it may be that your staffs have failed to manage your customers. Have you considered your cashiers and their level of operations? Is your bank a place people enter with joy and leave in sadness, because of your poor customer service?

A bank is just like hospital, in the sense that, while people go to the hospital to check their physical health, people go to banks because of their financial health, so you can imagine what your reaction would be, when you go to the hospital, and instead of being attended to, you get insulted by the receptionist, who tells you that, your file is missing, and that, the doctor is not on seat. You know this could threaten your life. So is a bank, whose customer care representatives, care-less while the managers have little regards for their small customers.

Your bank is at the verge of collapse, when it treats some customers as small, and others as big. Fine, there are obviously, customers, whose funds are needed to keep the bank viable. Such deserves attention, but not at the expense of the so-called "small customers". They all deserve equal attention. Let's take a cue from bank A. Bank A was a very big bank a few years ago, but today is ailing, why? Customers meant little or nothing to the members of staff of that bank. The bank was big and rich, but that wealth has now disappeared. The sad truth is that, a good number of the customers, the bank had displeased and discarded in the past, have embraced other banks and finds no reason to return to a bank; which did not value them in the first place.

Inefficiency is killing a lot of banks today. This is quite obvious, when the staff (rather than, do the job assigned them), are busy trying to protect their jobs. This, they do as they work under fear. So, rather than, attending to as many customers as possible, they spend the time they would have spent on two or more customers, attending to one customer. This inefficiency is also a function of limited gadgets. An example is the cash counting machine. The question is: Should a faulty counting machine be left sitting on the cashier's desk? That does not portray a serious bank. When two or three cashiers share one counting machine, this is bound to cause delay and thus displease customers.

It has become a norm in some banks that, there must be endless queues in the banking hall, regardless of the fact that, we are now in this era where things are done with pace and precision. If your bank is causing avoidable delays, it means that your bank is ailing.

What about financial predators and their impacts? Who are those handling your cash transfers, IT and other related services? How often do they undergo metal examination? More banks have become bankrupt as a result of IT related crime. Cases abound, where customers' funds have been infringed upon, through, minor deductions done in several accounts, a situation that, enriches the predators at the expense of the account holders.

A bank should be assessed, not by its brand, staff strength, physical structures and outlook, but by its financial positioning in the economy. As you well know, some of these outlooks are smoke screens. In recent times, we have seen lots of these so-called successful banks, declared bankrupt by regulatory authorities. So, what does this portray to the public? Nothing, other than, a smoke screen!

One major killer that has infiltrated a lot of banks are the killer marketers – a function of unrealistic targets. When marketers are sent out to the street to do the job of magicians, of course they would perform the magic, but the truth is that the customers they bring in initially may not be real. It is like the tricks in magic. What you see are illusions. Your bank is just like a passage where money disappears as they come. The reason is that, what your marketers have succeeded in doing is to get you more money and fewer customers. But the truth is that, you need more of customers than money. So when you set unrealistic monetary target, and your marketers meet that monetary obligation, they have only succeeded in chasing after money in the short run. Would it not have been better to set a realistic target, and get both the customers and their money instead of getting only the money, in the short run? Yes, you could get a customer and yet, not his money.

I once heard a marketer telling a prospective customer: "Don't worry, just open an account with us". This statement only shows one thing – that, the target is to get customers, and not to give value in exchange for patronage. This is a poor way of doing business. Please, note that, if you run your bank well, it will do well. If you observe those that are doing well in the banking business, you would observe that, one of the reason they stand out is because they offer quality services that are customer-friendly. Follow that lead!

Chapter Three: The Killing of Schools

We are in an era, where schools at all levels, are being set up. The need for educating people has necessitated this upsurge. Illiteracy faces its greatest challenge this period. UNICEF is doing a lot in the third world to combat illiteracy. Governments of countries, the world over, are investing in education. Individuals have also taken a cue – to invest in education, not only because they want to join the crusade, but for profitability. It is no secret that the setting up of schools is a great business. Private universities, now, are more in number than, ever before. So, the business is flourishing – a situation where demand seems greater than supply.

From the economic perspective, a business that has a story of demand that is greater than supply has the prospect of thriving. It is more, of a function of availability of capable and willing consumers (or customers). So, all that needs be done, is to increase out-put. The educational sector is at that point, where demand exceeds supply. But in spite of that, a lot of schools are still ailing, and some have, in fact, folded up! So what could be responsible for this situation in the midst of plenty? Why would a school die, or what are the things that could kill a school? You need to know these things before you enter into that line of business, so as to rescue your school from imminent collapse. For some personal reasons, I may not mention the names of some schools that were killed, but would rather analyze how and why they died.

It is a well known fact, that, the measure of the success of any school is proportional to the extent of success of the students. This measure is the reason for the death of many schools, whose authorities are trying to meet up with such standards. They would do everything – including wrong things, to portray their school in good light. In simple terms, the quest for success has resulted in the death of so many schools, a situation where those in authority, whose duty, it is, to enforce high standards, are the very ones now promoting substandard education and cutting corners – as long as it would result in a type of success that places the school in glowing light, publicly. Instances abound, where teachers disclose answers of examination questions to students. Some even apportion grades to students – all aimed at depicting the teacher, as one that is successful.

Interestingly, an analysis was made on this in *Freakconomics* by Steven D. Levitt and Stephen J. Dustner, when analyzing the issues on cheating and why teachers cheat and aid students to cheat. Here is an extract from the book:

"The stakes are considered high because instead of simply treating student to measure their progress, schools are increasingly held accountable for the results…. Twenty states rewarded individual schools for good test scores or dramatic improvement, thirty two states sanctioned the schools that didn't do well?"

This trend of reward-for-success and punishment-for-failure is one of the major causes of the death of not only, schools, but the educational system, as a whole. There are instances where teachers, in trying to save face, cheat, by aiding their students to attain high scores. The consequences of this act can only temporarily be concealed. With time, this is exposed, when such students face the true tests of their abilities. At this point, they fail woefully.

I had a relation that withdrew her children from a particular school, due to poor performance. Mind you, some of these schools are depicted as high flyers, but unfortunately, the products of such schools are failures. These are the ones that go to higher institutions, or other schools and fail to meet minimal academic standards. Schools are dying, because the authorities and teachers aid and abet cheating. And apart from this, students in such settings are unruly. Tell me, how do you control a student, whom you have encouraged to cheat? The answer is obvious.

A lot of schools have been shut down, because of acts of cheating, and a lot are ailing and as such, some parents are pulling their wards from such schools. Now, even when, such schools are not physically shut down, the performance of the graduates from that school is a sure sign that the school had long declined, academically. One thing, school owners and authorities should note, is that, their students are their products, and that, their performance, after, they graduate from the school, is a measure of the success, or failure of the school. So, when most of the products of a school are not doing well, such a school is not only ailing, but dead!

Another sure sign of the death of a school is indiscipline. The world is fast changing, and so, are trends, but that should not make one run a school without enforcing discipline. I overhead someone recently, who said: "Don't blame the child for being indiscipline; blame the parents, because lots of parents have thrown discipline to the dogs." Assuming this statement represents how you feel about the situation, the question would be: Have you also thrown discipline to the dogs, because you feel parents are to blame? Mind you, those parents, who were accused of throwing discipline to the dogs, eventually, withdrew their children and wards from your school, on the grounds that, your school has made their situation, twice, as worse.

It is puzzling to note, that, indiscipline is so indiscriminate in lots of school. Take note, that, it is more rampant in private schools, where students absent themselves from classes and attend parties, unnoticed. In fact, a lot of such schools create access for their students, to both misbehave, and be unruly. The outcome is usually failure. Incidentally, when such schools are threatened, by failure, they provide shortcuts for their students to cheat. It is therefore, not surprising, that, after such student(s) graduate from their respective schools, many of them fail to cope in the society – they reflect the failure of their schools.

In recent time, the act of cheating and failure rate of students has killed lots of schools. It is so obvious, as no sane parent, or guardian would want to send his child, or ward to such a school. Incidentally, a lot of such schools have died, as a result of lack of students. In the same vein, the physical structure of a school has ruined a lot of schools. Such school owners, have failed to perceive that, image creates impression. Thus, a depleting school structure reflects, a depleting school image – a sure sign of distress. A lot of schools are poorly maintained, and this is, sending wrong signal to the public.

Fine, you may decide to discard public impression, what about the students and their parents? The physical structure of your school is wrongly impacting on their pride, and if they have the slightest opportunity, they would take their leave from your school.

What about the library? A school without a library or a poorly serviced library is like an army that goes to warfare without ammunitions, or a farmer that, goes to the farm without farming implements. Failure abounds in a school without a library. A lot of schools have exited the stage, because of their failure to provide these facilities.

Chapter Four: The Killing Zone

There is a territory; there is an arena; there is a state; there is a stage; there is a zone in that any business that reaches it would be killed. So, you need to know this zones, so as to avoid them; to know if your business is heading in that direction; to know if your business is already in the trap, so that, you start preparing its funerals, exit, or escape. You need to know the likely traps, before commencing your business.

I love the lesson I had on temperature, while in secondary school. One key word struck me, and has stayed with me through the years. It is the term 'boiling point'. There is also, 'melting point'. The distinction was made with reference to water. I understood that it is, when you heat water and it reaches one hundred degree centigrade (100°C) in temperature, it has attained its boiling point. At that point, it starts to evaporate. Likewise, when you make it go through the cooling process, it eventually attains zero degrees centigrade (0°C). At that point, it becomes very cold and begins to freeze. These are illustrative of business processes and principles. That means that there is a point (zone) a business would attain that would yield it profits. Likewise, there is also a level that portends loss and failure and eventual death. In other words, there are zones of 'death' in the business world, and you need to know these zones, so as to safeguard your business from imminent death.

Characteristics of the Killing Zone

1. **Bigger Than Customers:** When a business becomes so successful or big that, it becomes bigger than its customers, that business has entered the zone of death.

You may then wonder how one knows, when his business is taking the ridiculous 'bigger-than, customer' outlook. To know this, find out, whether, this is a reflection of how your customers are serviced. The path of wisdom, in business requires that, there is the need for you to clinically analyze your business (from its inception), and determine, whether your response patterns (as regards customer relations), have been above board. When you sight customers, do you approach them, or wait for them to approach you? Do you render them, immediate assistance, before they ask for it? Do you smile at them, not minding that, you are yet to record any profit from the perceived transactions, with those sets of customers? If you do all these, then it means that, you elevate your customers higher, than your business.

With the aforementioned, your business has grown. It has grown so much, that, either you, or your staff fail to realize the presence of a customer. By this attitude, you have become so big, that, you can afford to tell a customer that, they are not wanted, even at the risk of boldly telling them that, you have more than enough. You even, filter your customers, and have created a grading system, by which you turn back some of your customers (directly, or indirectly), by ignoring them.

Let me tell you a story that would reverse this killer attitude, but first you must realize that, your business has died from the point you directly, or indirectly rate it, higher than your customers. Some years ago, information got to me about a booming restaurant's new policy. I learnt that, the restaurant took their customers through rigorous examination and assessment process, before they were allowed in. This process was imbibed, probably because of the high rate of patronage, and the thought that, the restaurant was exclusive to a certain class of persons. But, they failed to understand the secret of the success of that business, that, their low cadre customers remain the backbone of the business.

So, they had crafted that policy, and may have felt that, one of the best ways to access suitability and grant access into the restaurant was to assess the type of shoes one wore. That meant, that, if you visited that restaurant with a friend, or your partner and either you, or both of you, failed to meet their standard, access into the restaurant may be denied. I recall the experience I had at that restaurant some time ago. I had gone there with a friend. We were prepared financially to pick the bills, but we were disqualified from entering into the restaurant, based on their criteria. We had left there, disgusted.

This is the point to note: This trend, continued, until decay began setting in. In fact, at a point – apart from the door that was practically left ajar, for every Dick, Tom and Harry to freely enter – visitors were virtually, begged to patronize their services. As at now, that restaurant has folded up. It no longer exists!

Before the death of that restaurant, I had visited it severally. The symptoms of failure were obvious. The signs of decay – from their meals to their convenience – were obvious. The owners were responsible for that failure. They had thrown away "the baby with the bath water". There was no remedy to the imminent death of their business that, stared them in the face. There is a salient fact to note here, and that is, the fact that, by human nature, there is every tendency, to become complacent, when you tend to have achieved a measure of success. At that level, you tend to relax. But one thing, we fail to realize, is that, we got to where we are today, because we refused laxity access into our lives.

Your business may be doomed if it has grown bigger than your customers. One way to also detect this is the level and quality of attention your customers receive. Every customer deserves attention, and therefore, you don't attend to one customer and neglect another, because, you feel the one you are attending to, is superior to the other. You don't unnecessarily elevate one higher than another, by using a criterion, blurred by poor judgment.

Are you still wondering if your business has grown bigger than your customer, then consider, how often, either you, or your staff argue and quarrel with your customers. Of course, you can do that, because you know others would come, but mind you, one displeased **customer, is equivalent to several others. It is just a matter of time that business would die.**

2. **Bigger Than Maintenance:** Let's start again from when you started your business, that point, where you paid attention to every detail of your business affairs. You know, how much attention you gave your surroundings, tools and equipment. Does this still matter to you? Your business has entered the killing stage, if it has become so big, that, you have completely ignored, carrying out routine maintenance of your structures.

You may manage to still retain customers – the old customers may remain, but remember that the success of a business goes beyond the retention of old customers. It also includes, attraction of new customers, the frequency of which, leads to expansion. But then, how can you attract new customers, when you have turned your business into one that is old? Here is the point to note: the depleting customers, or the decrease in the influx of new customers is a likely outcome of your depleting structures! And perhaps, one reason for retaining such posture could be as a result of an erroneous thought that, what matters is your business moving forward, and that, you can survive, no matter the state of your structures. But you may have failed to realize that, the height your business has attained was as a result of the maintenance culture you imbibed in the past. Your business is in the death zone, when you start neglecting the maintenance culture you imbibed, when you newly started out in business.

This segment is a very serious segment, on the grounds that, it may be that, you are not aware that, your business is doomed to fail as you still assume that, you still have your regular customers coming. The essence of this book is to prevent possible business crash – a reason, why a lot of businesses that once thrived in the past, are no more operational. They had died, because the owners were blind to the consequence of rejecting maintenance culture. So you need to carry out routine checks, of your environment, equipments and be sure that they are properly serviced and maintained. Let me proceed, by recalling the last quote in chapter 12

"Your business depends on your structure, keep it working, and keep it clean. MAINTENANCE IS MANAGEMENT."

The phrase I want you to consider here is: "maintenance is management". The cost of neglecting maintenance culture is greater, than the cost of management, and this is evident, when you consider a vehicle that is regularly used and is rarely maintained. The owner may save cost in the short run, but in the long run – when the vehicle eventually breaks down – he may lose the vehicle completely, or may end up spending huge sum of money repairing it. And of course, he may never be able to get it to the state it would have been, had he been maintaining it as at when due. So is business.

That your production and output is on the rise does not mean your business is profitable. As long as your equipments are not properly maintained, the consequence is that, a breakdown may occur that might gulp not only your profit, but your investments.

Again, you don't want to create a wrong impression in the minds of your customers that, you are careless about your business. It is however, important to point out that, you would be creating such impression, when they notice the way you treat your tools and equipment, and as you know, **you don't expect people to treat your property better than you do. So, if you treat your property carelessly, people will help you do the same. If you ignore your properties, people would vandalize them. If you maintain your property poorly, people will resent you for doing that.** Your business is in the death zone, if your attitude or that of your staff is that of "the bigger than maintenance".

3.   **Nest of Creditors and Debtors:** Have your business become the mid-point between creditors and debtors? That is a sure sign that, it is in the death zone. You should always, and at all time of your operations, recall, how you started. Let's examine two scenarios:

First, did you start your business on loan? If so, have you been able to offset the loan? It is sad to note that, quite a number of establishments have been so blinded by the profit they seem to be making, while failing, to either pay back their loan, or make attempts to do same. Such a business has failed, if, despite the portrayal of grandeur, it displays, its debts are not being serviced.

Secondly, bad as the aforementioned may be, but is your business always surrounded by debtors? Is your business, at the point of decline, not because you did not meet up production, or sales was not recorded, but because most of the transactions done, were done on credit? Check out your books and note this fact that, your business is at the death zone.

It grieves me when I come across business owners, who complain of not making profit, all because of debtors. What you hear from them is: "If only "A" pays my money…., or "When would you pay my money?" Worse of them all, is the heart cry: "All my money are outside". **Here in is what I have learnt: It is better to hold on to your money, than to be involved in a business with debtors – the sorrow is endless.**

Finally, is your business sitting between the two evils of debtor and creditors? If so, it is at the death zone. The signs are obvious – **you spend a greater part of your time wishing to pay your creditors, and more of that time, hoping that, your debtors would pay you.** If this is your case, then you are in real trouble. The truth is that, your business is ailing. In fact you don't have a business. What you have is trouble!

WHEN YOUR BUSINESS IS ALWAYS BETWEEN CREDITORS AND DEBTORS, YOU DON'T HAVE A BUSINESS, WHAT YOU HAVE IS TROUBLE

Yes you have trouble, because you have surrounded yourself with problems. You don't have; you are in debt; you are being owed… what a terrible state to be - the death zone.

4. **Loads of Litigation:** Someone may say that, you cannot run a business without litigation. Unfortunately, I do not believe that notion. However, assuming, it is correct, why run your business in endless litigations?

Someone, even you may not be doing something right. If you study some companies' end of year reports, payments for litigations and outstanding litigations might make you wonder, if such a company is a law firm. Of course, we know that, law firms handle a lot of cases, but your business is not a law firm, then, it should not operate like one. So, why saddle it with a lot of court cases.

If your business is so characterized, it is obviously in the death zone. No business thrives on endless litigations, so, why is yours saddled with lots of litigations? You need to do something about the root causes, before it kills your business.

5. **Staff Exits:** Your staffs are resigning (old and new) and you think all is well? no I don't think so. You have failed to consider the cost involved.

    You lose a competent staff - one you have spent so much in training - and then replace him with another staff that you would spend so much to train (who eventually may leave), because what made staff A to leave, would obviously affect and make staff B leave too.

    The reason for the fluctuation in your business output and profitability may not be far from the fact that you have unstable employees.

    Your business is certainly at the killing zone if it is affected by repeated staff exits, this may not be immediately evident in your services, output and profit, but over time the result would show, but by then it would be too late - the reason quite a number of businesses die suddenly .

    Here's how this works, your thriving business may be on past jobs done and not necessarily on what is being done presently, so you may still be enjoying the yield of past labour, the profit may be regular, customers may still be coming, unknown to you that their response is not to what you are presently doing but the response are to the seed sown in the past. Then suddenly profits starts depleting, you begin to wonder why? You need not to think too far, examine the rate of exits of your employees, you might be lucky to rescue your business from the killing zone.

6. **Refund on Goods and Services:** Are your goods and services being returned and refunds are being requested for; if so your business is in the killing zone.

I love companies like Toyota, a very superb brand, this is a very successful company which did not wait for its customers complain or request for refund before the management swung into action. I recall the news sometime in 2010 how the company recalled millions of one of its brand of cars. Because of a flaw that was detected this was done at their expense.

Here lies the point, you can imagine a scenario where you hear that those that purchased that vehicle worldwide have been complaining about that car, but rather than waiting for such, the company swung into action and nobody heard much afterwards about what happened.?

Let's bring this back to your business, you have sold out a particular product, then followed certain complaints from customers, instead of swinging into action, you are just there waiting for more complaints. What you have failed to realize is that you are doing that at the peril of your business, the reason being that you are portraying your business in a wrong light. You are also creating the impression in the minds of people that it is not only that particular product that is bad, but the others and even those you are yet to produce may be so bedeviled.

The continuous refund of goods and services depicts a business on the killing zone. If it is a supermarket or grocery store you should be rest assured that a lot of people will stop patronizing you.

It is not a crime to have a product with defect, it becomes a crime not only when your customers repeatedly return and request for refund, but you fail to take action to avert the creation of a negative impression about your goods and services.

It is no big deal for you to go public and own up that there was a flaw with such goods and services, people will understand you and respect your courage. For it is better you own up before you are castigated. One thing I am sure of, I don't think the image you are trying to protect is as big as that of Toyota, and you need to take a cue from that successful company. No one not even a business is greater than mistakes.

NO ONE NOT EVEN A BUSINESS IS GREATER THAN MISTAKES.

You have seen some stage in which when your business attains, it is at the mercy of business killers, the insight given are tools to use in assessing the state of your business. **It is well advised that whatsoever thing, person, habits, tools that is rearing its head in your business that bears the mark of a killer, it is a sign that your business is in the killing zone and needs rescue. What you need to do is to examine the path it took to get to that stage and then make all the necessary adjustments.**

Part 4: The Last Business

Insight

"To everything there is a season, and a time to every purpose under the heaven. A TIME TO BE BORN, AND A TIME TO DIE.............." (Ecclesiastes 3:1, 2).

This is where we are starting "a time to be born and a time to die" something was not mentioned between the two extremes in that passage, which is "live", between our birth and death is our "living" and if you have been critical with the analysis given in part one and part two, you would observe the equivalence made between living and business- living in itself is business- it is only the living that conducts businesses.

The inference therefore from the aforementioned is that business ends at death; if this is accurate that means the analysis given in chapter 2 of part one "The death of the first business" is not conclusive, because though the first business died, it was a partial death, in that the structure put in place to sustain it are still there, the products from the first business are still there and alive.

The confirmation of that fact are the subsequent chapters that followed that analysis; all the activities analyzed are activities being carried out by the offspring of the first business of which I am one, and all the components established to sustain that business are still in place- oxygen, the earth, water, vegetables and other organisms are still on a notable scale in operation.

That business has in a large extent continued to achieve one of its mandate "be fruitful and multiply and replenish the earth". So we have one man's offspring sprang to over six billion people in a quest to replenish the earth, a mandate which to a large extent met the desire of the business Owner.

The question therefore is "can we say the business Owner is satisfied with this business progress?" The only person that can proffer answer to that query is the owner of the business.

So what I shall do is to access some of his programme for this business, and what may soon become of this business. These analyses are necessary for us, so that we may also take into cognizance that the environment within which we conduct our business is another's business and he has total right with what to do with it. Aside these, we are also his business and he has total right to do with us as he please. No marvel He declared through one of his messengers:

"Oh man, who art thou that repliest against God? SHALL THE THING FORMED (MAN) SAY TO HIM THAT FORMED IT (MAN), WHY HAST THOU MADE ME THUS?" (Romans 9:20).

So we have little to do about how the Owner of this business has decided to handle it, but one good thing about him is that he has made clear from time past how he intends this business to come to an end, and this is what I term the last business. What is the last business all about and what would happen? These are some of the things you shall soon be acquainted with. So that you also would align your business time table with his and get prepared for THE LAST BUSINESS.

Follow His lead, because you cannot afford to neglect what would happen to the environment in which you run your business.

Chapter One: The Last Business

There is hardly anybody who does not know that one day he would end his life's business in death. So we shall one day die, and this has been the trend right from the creation of the first man - a life span was determined by God for us - live and die.

That was the position he eventually found his main product, and since the fall of Adam in the garden there have been several births accompanied by commensurate deaths.

But if you may recall, man was just an aspect of God's business so the verdict of death was not only incurred by man, it was also incurred by the other components of the business, the earth included. The question therefore is that what would happen to the earth and all that are in and on it?

It is very important for you as a business man or woman to understand certain things about this space you conduct your business, so that you could also schedule your timetable to align with that of the owner of the space. For you would agree with me that there is an owner and if that be the case, there is need to know his intention for his business. This concern is necessary, so that one would not be taken unaware.

History also makes us to understand that our fore parents were taken unawares because they ignored aligning themselves and the timetable of their business with that of the Owner of the business they transact. They had ignored his complaints, warnings and consequent decision to close his business.

Of course you have the right to close your business, how much more God. So there is no basis to doubt what would happen to his business, and as it is, it is his business and whatsoever he decides with it so be it.

Back to our fore fathers on the shunning of the warnings given by the Owner of this business-God at their time got real angry about his business and decided to put an end to it.

"And the LORD said, I will destroy man whom I have created from the face of the earth, both man, and beast, and the creeping things, and the fowls of the air, for it repented me that I have made them (**established this business)".** Genesis 6:7.

Here was God's position with regard to his business at the instance mentioned above, his expectation of man and his business was not met, he soon realized that though his business was bound to die at certain point such position was not satisfactory to him, so he decided to completely shut down the business- the earth must be cleared of all living things".

Somehow that decision was upturned: Noah, seven members of his family and a few creatures escaped that destruction, the reason you are reading this book. So, what next?

A final verdict has been placed not only on man, but on the earth and universe. You need to get yourself acquitted with this verdict, because an acquaintance with this verdict will not only save your financial business, it will preserve your life's business.

An acquaintance with this verdict would also avail you the opportunity to run your business in a way that is acceptable to your Maker, because one thing you already know you can alter his impression about you and your life`s destiny, including your life`s business.

You may now wonder what we are getting at; we are headed at the direction our fore parents were about six thousand years ago, at that instance eight people were rescued, in our instance the verdict is quite different. Why, you may ask? I don't have an answer.

Maybe we should consider God's own query first, which may produce the answer to that.

"WHAT COULD HAVE BEEN DONE MORE TO MY VINE YARD (MAN AND OTHER CREATION), THAT I HAVE NOT DONE IN IT? Wherefore, when I looked that it should bring forth grapes, brought it forth wild grapes." Isaiah 5:4

Here was God after due diligence of his business, the out-put (yield) was not commensurate with the investment. So the question he asked was, what could have been done, was done to this business, but the outcome falls short of the investment- he is running at loss.

Yes God's business is not giving him the necessary satisfaction. Let`s pause here and retrospectively look at all the analyses given on business killers. One phrase you know was commonly used is that the very reason of entrants into a business is for profitability and sustainability; you know that any business that falls short of that has failed and should be closed. And if this is the way we view business, what about God? His business output is not commensurate with his investment, so he plans to do something.

"And now go to, I will tell you what I will do to my vineyard (man and the creation): I will take away the edge thereof, and it shall be eaten up; and break down the wall thereof, and it shall be trodden down". Isaiah5:5.

Something is clear about this declaration; this business of his is destined to be shut down, for it has fallen short of his expectation. This time there is no allowance, both living and none living (man, the earth and the universe) would be affected.

"THUS SAITH THE LORD OF HOSTS (GOD); YET ONCE, IT IS A LITTLE WHILE AND I WILL SHAKE THE HEAVENS, AND THE DRY LAND; AND I WILL SHAKE ALL NATIONS."Haggai 2:6-7.

This matter is getting out of hand, it is not going to be an earthquake, the heavens would quake too, and the whole universe would be shaken. Then what follows?

"LIFT UP YOUR EYES TO THE HEAVENS, AND LOOK UPON THE EARTH BENEATH: FOR THE HEAVENS SHALL VANISH AWAY LIKE SMOKE, AND THE EARTH SHALL WAX OLD LIKE A GARMENT, AND THEY THAT DWELL THERE IN SHALL DIE IN LIKE MANNER...BUT MY SALVATION SHALL BE FOR EVER AND MY RIGHTEOUSNESS SHALL NOT BE ABOLISHED." Isaiah 51:6.

The earth and the universe are shaken, and then suddenly they shall be no more. What about man?

"They that dwell therein shall die in like manner"- The last business is total annihilation of man and his environment. But if you critically examine this verdict, there is a clause that should be of interest to you:

"BUT MY SALVATION SHALL BE FOREVER, AND MY RIGHTEOUSNESS SHALL NOT BE ABOLISHED".

Where would this be? It tells us that God has other plans, that this total extermination would not affect those who have run their business in tune with God's instruction, those that have heeded his call for a new life; while this earth in which we presently live is wiped-out. God has special provision for the hereafter- one for those who neglect his call to change and repentance, and the other for those who heeded the call, embraced it and REPENTED.

For those who have led a wicked business life, the verdict:

THE WICKED SHALL BE TURNED INTO HELL, AND ALL NATIONS THAT FORGET GOD" Psalm10:17.

For those who remembered God in all their dealings, embraced his Salvation and led a righteous business life, the verdict-:

"FOR BEHOLD, I CREATE NEW HEAVENS AND A NEW EARTH: and the former shall not be remembered, nor come into mind" Isaiah 65:17

It is in this new heaven where they that have embraced salvation and the righteousness of God are to remain forever and not be abolished, and dwell with no remembrance of this present universe.

THIS IS THE LAST BUSINESS!

The End

We have come to the end of another business with focus on business killers, how to detect them, prevent them, rescue ones business from their grip and above all, how oneself can be rescued from the impending danger the earth and the inhabitants faces in Another's business.

BUSINESS KILLERS ARE ALL AROUND US, IN US, AND ONE DAY, JUST ONE DAY THE END SHALL BE UNVEILED!!

CLOSED

www.ingramcontent.com/pod-product-compliance
Lightning Source LLC
Chambersburg PA
CBHW070315190526
45169CB00005B/1637